Corvette

Tom Benford
Photography by James Mann

MOTORBOOKS

Dedication

For my loving wife, Liz, who shares my passion for America's Sports Car—the Corvette.
–Tom Benford

First published in 2007 by Motorbooks, an imprint of MBI Publishing Company LLC, Galtier Plaza, Suite 200, 380 Jackson Street, St. Paul, MN 55101 USA

Text © 2007 by MBI Publishing Company
Photography © 2007 by James Mann and Tom Benford

The information in this book is true and complete to the best of our knowledge. All recommendations are made without any guarantee on the part of the author or Publisher, who also disclaim any liability incurred in connection with the use of this data or specific details.

This publication has not been prepared, approved, or licensed by General Motors.

We recognize, further, that some words, model names, and designations mentioned herein are the property of the trademark holder. We use them for identification purposes only. This is not an official publication.

Motorbooks titles are also available at discounts in bulk quantity for industrial or sales-promotional use. For details write to Special Sales Manager at MBI Publishing Company, Galtier Plaza, Suite 200, 380 Jackson Street, St. Paul, MN 55101 USA.

To find out more about our books, join us online at www.motorbooks.com.

ISBN-13: 978-0-7603-2987-0
ISBN-10: 0-7603-2987-7

Editor: Lindsay Hitch
Designer: Sara Holle

Printed in China

About the Author: Tom Benford is a dyed-in-the-wool car guy, award-winning automotive writer, and historian. He has authored several books, including Motorbooks' *Corvette: Five Decades of Sports Car Speed*, *Corvette Performance Projects 1968–1982*, *The Street Rod*, and *Garage and Workshop Gear Guide*. Benford resides with his wife, Liz, in Brick Township, New Jersey. The Benford automotive stable includes six Corvettes from 1963 through 1998 and a 1933 Dodge five-window coupe street rod.

James Mann is a UK-based automotive photographer for the editorial and advertising industries. His work appears among the pages of top magazines all over the world, and he has contributed to more than 30 books; this is his fifth on Corvettes. He is the author of *How to Photograph Cars*, which was also published by MBI.

Credits: Photography copyright James Mann unless otherwise noted.

On the spine: 1959 Corvette

On the cover: (*main*) 1960 Corvette (*inset*) 1969 Corvette, 1967 Corvette, 2001 Corvette

On the frontispiece: 1962 Corvette

On the title pages: 1985 Corvette

On the back cover: 1967 Corvette, 1973 Corvette, 2006 Corvette

Library of Congress Cataloging-in-Publication Data
Benford, Tom.
    Corvette / by Tom Benford ; photography by James Mann.
        p. cm.
    Includes index.
    ISBN-13: 978-0-7603-2987-0 (softbound)
    ISBN-10: 0-7603-2987-7 (softbound)
    1. Corvette automobile—History. I. Title.
TL215.C6.B4496 2007
629.222'2—dc22
                                2007004853

Contents

Introduction

THE NATIONAL CORVETTE MUSEUM

Corvette

Every car starts with an idea and a vision, sometimes that of a sole individual. In the case of the Corvette, that individual was Harley Earl, the head of styling at General Motors.

It was 1951 and Earl was impressed by a sports car competition rally he attended in Watkins Glen, New York. Sports cars were popular with returning GIs after World War II who had gotten acquainted with the low, nimble, and fast European two-seaters during their tours of duty. These cars impressed Earl so much that he was determined to create a new breed of American car that could compare favorably with Europe's Jaguars, MGs, Alfa Romeos, and Ferraris. His goal was to have a stylish two-seat convertible design ready for the company's January 1953 Motorama exhibition at the prestigious Waldorf-Astoria Hotel in New York City. These Motorama exhibitions were events GM ran from 1949 through 1961 that visited major cities and were open to the public. Used to showcase new models and styling ideas, the shows gauged public interest and gathered feedback about the proposed new models.

There was a general feeling of optimism throughout the country at the time thanks to the recent American victory of World War II. The United States was the best place on Earth to live, and life here was *great*. After hunkering down during the war years, the American public was eager for new and better products, including automobiles. Folks were ready to see things that would bring smiles to their faces. And by that time, Harley Earl was already working on a car that would make hearts thump, quicken pulses, and produce ear-to-ear grins.

The prototype roadster was secretly developed in Earl's private studio at GM. While its official designation was "EX 122" (EX denoting its experimental status), it was referred to under the code name of "Opel." Earl wanted the car to have a name beginning with "C" since it was going to be showcased as part of the Chevrolet lineup at the General Motors Motorama, but he didn't want it to be the name of an animal. Myron Scott, a photographer for GM's advertising agency, came up with the suggestion of "corvette," which described a

small, fast, and maneuverable warship that had functioned as a destroyer escort during the war.

The Corvette "dream car" was an immediate hit at the show—nothing even remotely like it was being offered by any other domestic or even foreign car maker. Pleased with the great public reception it received, GM management gave the fiberglass roadster its blessing and the green light to start manufacturing at Chevrolet's Flint, Michigan, plant.

And so it all began. Who would or could have guessed that this little two-seater would become a true world-class sports car destined to dominate racetracks, rule the streets, and be Chevrolet's longest continually produced nameplate?

1953–1962

Chapter 1

You could get the new 1953 Corvette in any color you wanted, as long as it was Polo White with a Sportsman Red interior; a manually operated black canvas convertible roof and whitewall tube-type tires were also standard complements on the car. The Chevrolet script-style signature was affixed on each front fender above a long, slender trim strip with a spear-like hash that extended from the front to the rear wheelwell. In December 1953, production moved from Flint to a GM assembly plant in St. Louis, Missouri.

Only 300 Corvettes were built in 1953, and more than 270 survivors still exist today, commanding six figures on the collector car market when properly restored.

The 1954 Corvette was mostly a reincarnation of the 1953 model, but in addition to Polo White, exterior color choices also included red, blue, and black, as well as a beige color option for the convertible top. A new camshaft boosted the motor to 155 horsepower, up 5 from the previous year. Total production for 1954 was 3,640 Corvettes, although about one-third of them remained unsold at the year's end. Several Corvettes were given to celebrities, including Dave Garaway, John Wayne, and others, in a PR attempt to promote the car.

In 1955, the car got its first shot of mechanical testosterone. Zora Arkus-Duntov, an automotive engineer and former European road racer who was a part of the original Corvette task force, was determined to make Corvette turn the marketing corner. While outward appearances remained basically the same as the two previous years, the roadster began to exhibit true sports car performance with the introduction of Chevrolet's 265-cubic-inch Turbo-Fire V-8 engine coupled with an automatic choke, a 12-volt electrical system, and, in later models, a three-speed manual transmission. The new V-8-powered Corvette listed for $2,909, and only 700 units were produced in 1955. That same year, Ford introduced its V-8-powered two-seat Thunderbird, and competition for market share was on.

The Corvette's fiberglass body got a makeover in 1956 that would stay with it for the next several years. A sculptured, scooped-out

cove in the side of the car, trimmed by chrome, made clean two-tone color combinations possible. Plus, the car now had outer door handles with locks and roll-up windows.

The year 1957 saw additional performance modifications with the introduction of a new 283-inch V-8 equipped with fuel injection for the first time and a four-speed manual transmission. The base price of the car was $3,176, and a total of 6,339 units were sold—double the number of 1956 sales. The Corvette attracted a loyal following attesting to its appeal: the Northern California Corvette Club became the first of many clubs in the United States.

From 1958 through 1962, the Corvette continued to evolve in both performance and styling—subtle changes finessing the car with each new model year. The Corvette had become such a piece of Americana that a new television show, *Route 66*, debuted in October 1960 featuring two fellows and their adventures across the United States in their Corvette. The show aired through August 1964.

On June 30, 1953, the first Corvette rolled off the assembly line, powered by a vintage 235-ci Chevrolet straight-six overhead-valve engine that sported three single-barrel carburetors, dual exhausts, and a floor-mounted, two-speed Powerglide automatic transmission. Rechristened as the "Blue Flame Special," the engine generated 150 horsepower. Many of the other basic components of the car, however, were standard, tried-and-true, off-the-shelf items from Chevrolet's inventory.

Price: $3,734.55 (with options)

Engine: 235-ci straight-six, 150 horsepower

Transmission: Two-speed Powerglide automatic

Total production: 300

Fact: The first production Corvettes were literally pushed off the assembly line. They wouldn't start due to electrical grounding problems caused by the fiberglass body that hadn't been considered previously.

The profile of the 1953 Corvette showed off its low, sleek lines to best advantage. The little two-seater was unlike anything else produced by American auto manufacturers, or any other manufacturers, for that matter, and it caused a sensation.

The tried-and-true Chevrolet Stovebolt six was enhanced with three side-draft, single-barrel carburetors and dual exhausts to boost its output to 150 horsepower and was renamed the "Blue Flame Special" to power the new Corvette.

The gauges were centrally mounted on the lower half of the dashboard for a sporty, although none-too-practical, appearance. The radio speaker was mounted on the passenger side of the dash.

Only available as a convertible, the 1953 Corvette came equipped with a manually operated black canvas convertible top. It did not have any windows or exterior door handles.

Wide, whitewall tires were the order of the day to give the rolling gear some eye appeal.

Chromed-mesh stone guards covered the headlights.

To say the new sports model was sparsely equipped is no understatement; there were no exterior door handles (the doors opened from the inside), and plastic side curtains were used in place of windows. The $3,498 price tag of the basic 1953 roadster did not include the optional heater ($91.40 extra) or the AM radio (another $145.15), although all 300 of the production models were equipped with these options.

The Corvette was able to go from 0 to 60 miles per hour in a respectable 11 seconds, clock the quarter-mile in 18 seconds, and attain a top speed just shy of 110 miles per hour. Despite this, some industry pundits postulated that the Corvette was merely a GM styling experiment that would soon fade into oblivion. And that just proves how wrong experts can be sometimes.

Except for additional color choices and options, the 1954 Corvette was a carbon copy of the 1953 model.

Encouraged by the warm reception the Corvette had received in its inaugural year, the Chevrolet plant in St. Louis, Missouri, had been retooled to manufacture 10,000 Corvettes annually, but demand was misjudged . . . by a long shot.

A midyear camshaft modification increased the six-cylinder block's output to 155 horsepower, although the Powerglide two-speed automatic transmission remained standard. Exterior color options were expanded from basic Polo White to include Pennant Blue, Sportsman Red, and black in limited numbers;

Price: $2,774

Engine: 235-ci straight-six, 155 horsepower

Transmission: Two-speed Powerglide automatic

Total production: 3,640

Fact: Although the extra accessory items were said to be "optional," all 3,640 1954 Corvettes were equipped with them.

soft top roofs were also available in beige, and production-model tires were upgraded from tube-type to tubeless. The stainless-steel exhaust pipes, located low in the rear fascia, had a tendency to stain the paint finish, so they were

In 1954, factory air consisted of a pop-up vent that directed fresh outside air into the passenger compartment. True air conditioning would not become available for the Corvette until 1963.

The tips of the dual exhausts were lengthened to help alleviate soot marring the paint finish, a problem that became evident on 1953 models.

lengthened. The two-handle hood-latch release system used in the 1953 model proved cumbersome and was replaced by a single-release handle.

To help give sales a shot in the arm, the base price of the 1954 Corvette decreased to $2,774. Additional options for 1954 included windshield washers, whitewalls, directional signals, radio and heater, a parking brake alarm, and courtesy lights.

In 1954, Corvette production increased by a factor of twelve over 1953, resulting in 3,640 units being made; unfortunately, about one-third of these remained unsold at the year's end. The lofty production goal of 10,000 annual units wouldn't be achieved until 1960.

Aside from changes in the exterior badging and expanded color choices, the Corvette looked pretty much the same in 1955 as it did in the previous two years.

Zora Arkus-Duntov, an automotive engineer and former European road racer, was one of the early members of the Corvette task force and was determined to make Corvette turn the marketing corner through improvements in two main areas: handling and performance. It was through his efforts that the Corvette got its first shot of mechanical testosterone: the 265-ci Turbo-Fire V-8 engine, the first of what would become the legendary small-block Chevy V-8s.

While outward appearances remained basically the same as the two previous years, with this new engine the roadster began its evolution into true sports car performance. Other innovations for 1955 included an automatic choke, a 12-volt electrical system, and, somewhat later in the model year, a three-speed manual transmission.

Thanks to the new V-8, the Corvette could clock 0 to 60 miles per hour in just 8.5 seconds and rip the quarter-mile in 16.5 seconds. As if that wasn't enough, it could reach a top speed of nearly 120 miles per hour, and gasoline mileage improved about 2 to 3 miles per gallon over the Blue Flame's inline six.

The big news for 1955 was the 265-ci 195-horsepower Turbo-Fire V-8 engine.

Price: Six-cylinder, $2,774; V-8, $2,909

Engine: 235-ci straight-six, 155 horsepower; 265-ci V-8, 195 horsepower

Transmission: Two-speed Powerglide automatic; later in the year, a three-speed manual gearbox was also offered

Total production: 700

Fact: Only seven purchasers opted for the Blue Flame Special six-cylinder engine in 1955, attesting to the overwhelming success of the newly introduced 265-ci/195-horsepower V-8.

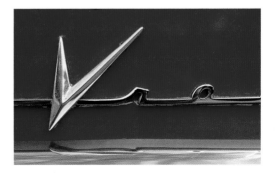

The pronounced "V" in the Chevrolet script clearly proclaimed to the world that a V-8 powerplant was under the hood of this Corvette.

The new cove sides introduced for the 1956 model would go on to become a Corvette trademark for the remainder of the marque's first generation.

For 1956, the Corvette fiberglass body underwent its first major styling change. A sculpted, scooped-out cove in the sides of the body was to become a Corvette trademark, and the chrome trim around the cove permitted two-tone color combinations for the first time. The headlights were moved forward and trimmed with chrome, the hood sported a pair of wind splits, and nonfunctional vent scoops adorned the top of each fender.

The rear fenders were contoured and followed the sloping rear deck, and the taillights were recessed above vertical chrome bumper guards. The persistent staining caused by the exhaust was alleviated by moving the pipes so they exited through the vertical bumper guards.

Price: $3,120

Engine: 265-ci V-8, 210 horsepower; 265-ci, 225 horsepower (2x4bbl. carbs)

Transmission: Three-speed manual, two-speed Powerglide automatic (optional)

Total production: 3,467

Fact: Zora Arkus-Duntov, driving a modified 240-horsepower, V-8-powered prototype during Speed Week trials, set a record of 150 miles per hour over Daytona's Measured Mile.

Other modifications included external door handles and locks, roll-up windows, optional power windows, and a hydraulically operated convertible roof. Options also available for the first time were factory-built auxiliary hardtops (in addition to white or beige soft tops) and seatbelts (available in kit form) from dealers.

Other new 1956 goodies included knock-off wheel covers, transistorized AM radios, adjustable passenger seats, a higher-output 12-volt battery system, and a new type of clutch for standard transmissions. Engine choices ranged from a basic 210-horsepower V-8 to a 225-horsepower with dual four-barrel carburetors. A special high-lift camshaft option—recommended "for racing purposes only"—unofficially rated the engine at 240 horsepower.

And, for the first time, the 1956 Corvette was called a "convertible" rather than the "roadster" designation it had for the previous three years.

Two four-barrel carburetors and an optional high-lift camshaft managed to pump an awesome 240 total horsepower out of the 265-ci small-block V-8, making the Corvette a serious contender when it came to performance.

The new styling for the 1956 Corvette added immense visual appeal to the car, and the addition of the chrome-trimmed cove sides made two-tone paint schemes possible.

The quintessential Corvette: an image of a two-tone cove-side Corvette like this black-and-silver '57 immediately comes to mind for many people.

Now in its fifth year of production, the "plastic fantastic" set another American milestone with the introduction of the 283-ci motor, as the evolution of the small-block Chevy V-8 engine continued.

The new 283, when teamed with such options as a four-speed manual transmission and fuel injection, achieved a surprising 283 horsepower—the magic goal of one horse-power per cubic inch of displacement. In so doing, the Corvette became one of the first cars in automotive history to marry fuel injection with four-speed manual shift.

Although 1957 body styling remained the same as 1956, handling was improved in selected models through a heavy-duty racing suspension, special front and rear springs and shocks, a heavier front stabilizer bar, and rear axle Posi-Traction, which endowed both rear wheels with power. Other performance-oriented innovations included finned brake drums, front brake air scoops, fresh air ducting to the rear brakes, and a mechanical tachometer mounted on the steering column. Now, the label "sports car" was truly more than just a catch term for marketing.

With fuel-injection-enhanced perform-ance, the 1957 was able to clock 0 to 60 in just 5.7 seconds and a quarter-mile in 14.3 seconds, and record a top speed of 132 miles per hour.

The front of the 1957 model was basically a carry-over of the styling used on the 1956 edition with no changes.

Price: $3,176.32

Engines: 283-ci/220-horsepower V-8

283-ci/245-horsepower V-8 (2x4 carburetors)

283-ci/270-horsepower V-8 (2x4 carburetors)

283-ci/250-horsepower V-8 (fuel injection)

283-ci/283-horsepower V-8 (fuel injection)

Transmission: Three-speed manual (close ratio), four-speed manual, two-speed Power-glide automatic

Total production: 6,339

Fact: In 1957, a Corvette won the 12 Hours at Sebring, the SCCA Class B/Sports, and SCCA Class B/Production Sports titles.

A variety of engine flavors was on the menu for 1957, starting with the basic 220-horsepower single four-barrel 283 V-8 and up to the fuel-injected 283-horsepower top-of-the-line option for the seriously power hungry.

Things were really starting to look up for the Corvette as the marque finally turned its first profit.

Chrome was the big new thing in 1958, and it was used extensively. Quad headlights (two on each side) trimmed with chrome connected to a chrome strip that ran back across the top of the fenders. Two simulated air ducts were located low in the front fenders, and larger bumpers were connected to the frame rather than the fiberglass body. Simulated vents were added to the coves behind the front wheelwells as well as twin chrome trunk strips. Up front, the Corvette's distinctive chrome grille was reduced from 13 teeth to 9, and some models came with hubcaps instead of wheel discs. Acrylic lacquer replaced enamel as the finish paint, and a hood with phony louvers (dubbed the "washboard" by its detractors) were the distinguishing features.

The body also grew, stretching 9 inches longer while it became more than 2 inches wider. This increase added 200 pounds, and the Corvette tipped the scales at almost 1.5 tons (2,960 pounds, to be exact).

The new features continued inside the cockpit with all of the instruments now centrally positioned directly in front of the driver, including a 160-mile-per-hour speedometer and a 6,000-rpm tachometer. Other new interior touches included a central console that housed the heater controls, clock, and signal-seeking AM radio. Seatbelts were also factory-installed for the first time.

The grille for the 1958 Corvette lost some teeth, down to 9 from the former 13, but there was still plenty of chrome eye candy to keep things looking bright.

Chrome straps adorned the trunk lid and helped to carry the bright-work theme through from the front of the car to the rear.

Price: $3,591

Engines: 283-ci/220-horsepower V-8

283-ci/245-horsepower (2x4 carburetor)

283-ci/270-horsepower (2x4 carburetor)

283-ci/250-horsepower (fuel injection)

283-ci/290-horsepower (fuel injection)

Transmission: Three-speed manual, four-speed manual, two-speed Powerglide automatic

Total production: 9,168

Fact: Corvettes continued to turn up the heat on the tracks when two Corvettes were entered into the Sebring Grand Prix of Endurance, making that the last road race with official factory participation. And Zora Arkus-Duntov, driving a Corvette SS, hit 183 miles per hour at GM's proving grounds in Arizona.

The restyled interior took on a more ergonomic, no-nonsense appearance with the addition of a center console and driver-grouped instrumentation.

The 1959 has the overall symmetry and good looks to make it a perennial favorite of classic Corvette collectors.

Nineteen fifty-nine was a year of modest growth for the Corvette, with production levels increasing by only 500 units from the previous year to 9,670. However, this was to be the final year that Corvette sales would be less than 10,000 units annually.

Gaudiness took a slight back seat to taste as some of the excessive chrome of the preceding year was eliminated. Pure black, blue, or turquoise interiors were available for the first time, supplementing the standard red, beige, and the occasional yellow or charcoal hues.

Additional interior changes included the repositioning of armrests and door handles to provide more elbow room. The dashboard gauges were also recalibrated, and concave lenses were utilized to cut down on light reflection and to improve readability. The four-speed manual transmission's new T-bar lockout on the shift handle prevented accidental shifting into reverse; this would become a long-lived standard feature on all Corvette (and Chevrolet) four-speed manual transmissions.

Spring rates were modified to accommodate the additional weight added with the 1958 model, and the rear shock absorber mounts were changed to provide a softer ride. Horizontal slits were added to wheel covers to improve brake cooling.

In tests, the 1959 Corvette roared from 0 to 60 in 6.6 seconds and ran the quarter-mile in 14.5 seconds.

Price: $3,875

Engines: 283-ci/230-horsepower V-8

283-ci/245-horsepower (2x4 carburetor)

283-ci/270-horsepower (2x4 carburetor)

283-ci/250-horsepower (fuel injection)

283-ci/290-horsepower (fuel injection)

Transmission: Three-speed manual, four-speed manual, two-speed Powerglide automatic

Total production: 9,670

Facts: Corvette once again won SCCA's Class B/Production Sports title and, at the official opening of the Daytona International Speedway, a Corvette was driven at 155 miles per hour. Also at this time, work began on the Chevrolet Experimental Racing Vehicle (CERV I).

The simulated air ducts behind the bumpers on the front of the Corvette were carry-over styling cues from the 1958 model. While they looked good, they were not functional.

The spring-loaded T-bar on the shifter handle prevented accidental shifts into reverse by locking out the reverse gear until the T was intentionally lifted using the index and middle fingers.

Very little was changed for the 1960 Corvette.

With 10,261 1960 Corvette convertibles rolling off the assembly line and out of showrooms, it was evident that the Corvette was now solidly established in the domestic automotive market.

Although the smooth contoured exterior was similar to the 1959 model, this was the last year for taillights molded into the rounded rear fenders, and the grille's teeth would also make their final appearance in 1960. A new metallic paint color, Cascade Green, made its debut in 1960.

Aluminum radiators with top expansion tanks made their appearance but were limited to the high-lift camshaft engines. Aluminum cylinder heads were used for the first time on

Price: $3,872

Engines: 283-ci/230-horsepower V-8

283-ci/245-horsepower (2x4 carburetors)

283-ci/270-horsepower (2x4 carburetor)

283-ci/250-horsepower (fuel injection)

283-ci/290-horsepower (fuel injection)

Transmission: Three-speed manual, four-speed manual, Powerglide automatic (carbureted engines only)

Total production: 10,261

Facts: Four Corvettes traveled to Europe to compete at Le Mans, where one finished fifth in the GT class and eighth overall. In SCCA Class B/Production racing, Corvette captured the points championship, edging out the second-place finisher: Ferrari. Corvette also captured the SCCA C/Modified championship.

Fuel-injected powerplants remained among the most popular options ordered for 1960, but they were only available with four-speed manual transmissions.

Nineteen sixty was the last year for taillights that were molded into the rear fenders, a sign of the new design winds blowing back at GM styling.

the high-performance fuel-injected models. The use of lighter-weight metals for a number of other components helped trim overall vehicle heft.

And, for the first time, all fuel-injected engines required manual transmissions, unlike previous years when automatic transmissions could be combined with lower-horsepower fuel-injected powerplants.

Meanwhile, back at R&D, the CERV I (the "R" now stood for Research, not Racing), a midengine, open-wheel, single-seat prototype racing model made its first public showing at Riverside International Raceway in California.

The boat-tail rear was a totally new styling cue for the 1961 Corvette, as the solid-axle era was nearing its end.

A 160-mile-per-hour speedometer and a 7,000-rpm tachometer let you know that there's plenty of power under the hood just waiting to be tapped.

The famous crossed-flags logo became a world-recognized symbol of the power, handling, and styling that are uniquely Corvette.

Nineteen sixty-one was a year of major styling changes that started at the rear of the Corvette. Adapted from the XP-700 show car, a "duck tail" or "boat tail" rear effect was lower and less rounded than preceding models and increased trunk space by about 20 percent. Other new rear end treatments included four recessed tail-lights, an innovation that became a Corvette trademark. The license plate was also recessed, flanked by chrome bumperettes.

Up front, the chrome surrounding the quad headlights was eliminated, as was the traditional toothy grille. It was also the last year for the contrasting two-tone side cove available since 1956 and the 283-ci engine that had been standard since 1957. There were power-boosting options, however, that generated 275 and 315 horsepower from the stock block. Also, the use of more aluminum components further reduced bulk weight.

Price: $3,934

Engines: 283-ci/230-horsepower V-8

283-ci/245-horsepower (2x4 carburetor)

283-ci/270-horsepower (2x4 carburetor)

283-ci/275-horsepower (fuel injection)

283-ci/315-horsepower (fuel injection)

Transmission: Three-speed manual, four-speed manual, Powerglide automatic (carbureted engines only)

Total production: 10,939

Fact: The 1961 Corvette was the last Corvette to retail for under $4,000.

The era of the two-tone, chrome-trimmed cove came to an end in 1962. Narrower whitewalls were also a popular option.

Production increased to 14,351 units and required a second shift at the factory. Engine displacement grew from the previous 283 to 327 cubic inches, with a maximum rating of 360 horsepower. Nineteen sixty-two would be the last year for conventional rear trunks, exposed headlights, optional power tops, two-tone paint jobs, and solid rear axles.

The optional Powerglide transmission now had an aluminum case to trim chassis weight. Four-speed manual transmissions remained popular options, accounting for better than 75 percent of the total units produced. Tachometers were driven by the distributor in all models, unlike previous years when tachs were limited to fuel-injected V-8 engines. Heaters were offered as standard equipment for the first time.

Price: $4,038

Engines: 327-ci/300-horsepower V-8

327-ci/340-horsepower V-8

327-ci/360-horsepower V-8 (fuel injection)

Transmission: Three-speed manual, four-speed manual, Powerglide automatic

Total production: 14,531

Fact: The 1962 Corvette was the last year of the "first generation" of Corvettes, or C1s as they are known. They have also been referred to as the "Glamour Years," defined by body styles rather than the model's basic platform.

Distributor-driven tachometers became part of the standard instrumentation for all models, regardless of engine output, in 1962.

Brightwork was also downplayed with the 1962 model, as evidenced by the black grille.

1963–1967

Chapter 2

Thanks to the continuing efforts of chief engineer Zora Arkus-Duntov to make the Corvette a world-class sports car, the Corvette Sting Ray premiered in 1963. For the first time in Corvette history, the marque was available both as a coupe and as a convertible. A totally new chassis equipped with independent rear suspension replaced the solid axle, endowing the car with outstanding handling. A new 327-ci engine was standard on the car, and performance options including a 360-horse-power fuel-injected version made the Sting Ray a force to be reckoned with on the track, while its sleek, sinewy beauty captivated onlookers on the street. Corvette stylist Larry Shinoda penned the immortal lines of the 1963 Sting Ray. The coupe, at the insistence of Bill Mitchell, had a separating strip on the rear window. Because it hampered rear visibility, this split strip was dropped for the 1964 model, making the 1963 Corvette Sting Ray split-window coupe the singularly most recognizable Corvette ever produced and a perennial favorite among collectors.

The new body styling introduced in 1963 carried through the 1967 model year and, though it only had a five-year run, its lines are timeless. These Sting Rays are known as "Mid-Years" and are arguably the most beautiful and sought after Corvettes of all time.

The 1964 coupe model did away with the split bar of the rear window and eliminated the decorative chrome grilles that appeared on the hood of the 1963 car. In 1965, minor styling changes were made to the body, but the big news was the availability of the big-block engine. The 1966 Corvette's styling copied its predecessors with only minor cosmetic changes. Backup lights became standard equipment, and hazard lights were optional. A 427-ci engine was introduced, and output was initially listed at 450 horsepower but rated downward (for insurance purposes) to 425 horsepower shortly thereafter.

For 1967, an all-new body style had been planned, but design and production problems delayed its introduction for another year. Nineteen sixty-seven was the last year for the Sting Ray body style introduced in 1963, making this final edition of the Mid-Years, especially the "bad boy" big-block versions, highly prized among collectors.

Nineteen sixty-three began the second decade of Corvette production and ushered in the next generation for the marque. The new Corvette received a total restyling treatment based on Chevrolet head of styling Bill Mitchell's 1959 Sting Ray race car. Now christened the Sting Ray, this fresh new look for the Corvette was available in both convertible and coupe versions and its stunning lines, penned by stylist Larry Shinoda, were breathtaking. The car received immediate public and critical acclaim.

Hideaway concealed headlights, offered for the first time, enhanced the lines of the softly pointed nose of the car when not in use (this feature became a Corvette trademark for the next 42 years until the 2005 C6 Corvette revived exposed headlights). An internal roll bar in the coupe contributed to additional frame rigidity and provided rollover protection for the passenger compartment as well.

Other innovative standard equipment for 1963 included independent rear suspension replacing the former solid axles, a shorter wheelbase (trimmed down to 98 inches from 102 inches), and a ladder-type frame with five crossmembers for better rigidity than the

The optional Kelsey-Hayes cast-aluminum knock-off wheels originally had some casting problems that caused air leakage; these wheels were offered a bit later in the 1963 model year as dealer-installed options after the leakage problems were ironed out. Nineteen sixty-six was the last year knock-offs were offered, as the DOT ruled them unsafe and dangerous due to their nasty habit of coming loose at highway speeds if not properly tightened and secured by retaining pins. *Tom Benford*

The soft nose of the 1963 Corvette, which started the Mid-Year era (1963–1967), sported faux chrome hood grilles and the hideaway headlights that would become a Corvette trademark for the next 42 years. *Tom Benford*

previous X-frame chassis. This redesigned chassis allowed passengers to ride comfortably inside the frame, rather than on top of it, endowing the car with a lower center of gravity for better handling and a lower, sleeker overall look.

In competitive racing circles, Corvette temporarily lost its SCCA edge to the Ford-powered, Carroll Shelby–developed Cobra, thanks to the latter's higher power-to-weight ratio. But, the Corvette Grand Sport recorded its first victory at Watkins Glen that summer, and, in the fall, a trio of specially prepared Grand Sports handily beat the Cobras in a series of races in Nassau.

Price: $4,257

Engines: 327-ci 250-/300-/340-horsepower V-8 or 327-ci 360-horsepower V-8 (fuel injected)

Transmissions: Three-speed manual (standard), four-speed manual syncromesh, two-speed Powerglide automatic

Total production: 21,513 (10,594 coupes)

Fact: A 36-gallon fuel tank was offered on coupes ($202.30 extra), intended as an option for racing. Known as "tankers," only 63 coupes were so equipped and now command premium prices among collectors.

Just over 2,600 Corvettes, both coupes and convertibles, were outfitted with the Powerglide two-speed automatic transmission in 1963, and many of these cars were also equipped with creature comforts such as power windows, power steering, and power brakes. *Tom Benford*

"Designer's Choice, Larry Shinoda" reads the autograph of the car's designer signed in permanent marker on the glove box door. Shinoda inscribed it for the author at the annual Corvettes at Carlisle show in Pennsylvania in August 1997, just two months before he died. *Tom Benford*

The sharp creases at the top of the bulging fenders gave the new 1963 Corvette Sting Rays a decidedly more-aggressive appearance while still being stylish.

For the first time since the Corvette's inception, neither the coupe nor the convertible had a trunk. The spare tire was cleverly stored and concealed in a fiberglass carrier basket that nestled between the dual exhausts just to the rear of the independent rear suspension's differential.

Acceptance of the new two-model lineup was immediate and overwhelming, with the demand exceeding the supply. Although a total of 10,919 convertibles and 10,594 coupes were turned out, many buyers had to wait several months for delivery and dealers didn't budge a penny off the sticker prices. Corvette annual production grew 50 percent, surpassing 21,500 units—another first for the marque.

The 1963 Corvette began the Mid-Year era, which only lasted through 1967, thought by many to be the glory years of the Corvette. The Mid-Years caused the Corvette to be recognized as a true world-class sports car and are the most highly cherished of all Corvettes due to their timeless styling and low production.

Price: $4,037 (convertible)

Engines: 327-ci 250-/300-/340-horsepower V-8 or 327-ci 360-horsepower V-8 (fuel injected)

Transmissions: Three-speed manual (standard), four-speed manual syncromesh, two-speed Powerglide automatic

Total production: 21,513 (10,919 convertibles)

Fact: A set of five Kelsey-Hayes aluminum knock-off wheels was initially offered as a factory option ($322.80), but casting problems caused the wheels to leak air. After these problems were solved, the knock-off wheels were offered later in the model year as a dealer-installed option.

Trunks, per se, were done away with for the Corvette starting with 1963 and wouldn't reappear until the C5 generation. The seats tilted forward to provide access to the storage area under the rear deck.

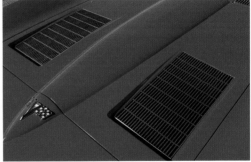

Nineteen sixty-three was the only year the faux hood-top trim panels would be used, although the recesses for them would be retained on the following year's hood.

Pleated upholstery on the bucket seats and chrome seat trim complemented other bright work found on the doors and center console, giving the Mid-Years a somewhat opulent appearance.

The controversial split of the rear window was removed for 1964, never to return again. Other than that, very little was changed from the 1963 model.

Very little was done to alter the 1964 Corvette's styling, although the split rear window feature was eliminated, replaced by a wraparound design. The relatively new coupes dropped from 1963's 10,594 to 8,304 units. Four engine options were available, with the top-of-the-line fuel-injected version now putting out 375 horsepower. A special front and rear suspension option package dampened bumps from rough roads without affecting handling. Additional insulation and better body and transmission mounts addressed noise complaints. A three-speed fan, added to improve ventilation in the rear of the coupes, drew fresh air from working vents located in the driver-side roof panel.

Many owners of 1963 Corvette coupes had the split bar of the rear window and the faux engine hood grilles removed in an effort to make them look like the new 1964 model. Conversely, a couple of decades later, the split bar was added to 1964 models in attempts to counterfeit them as '63 split-window coupes, which had subsequently become collector's models.

Price: $4,252

Engines: 327-ci 250-/300-/365-horsepower V-8 or 327-ci 375-horsepower V-8 (fuel injected)

Transmissions: Three-speed manual, four-speed manual syncromesh, two-speed Powerglide automatic

Total production: 22,229 (8,304 coupes)

Fact: While both sides of the coupe have them, only the driver-side rear vent of the 1964 Corvette is functional.

The arrangement of two taillights on each side surrounded by chrome bezels was used throughout the Mid-Year era.

In this frontal view, you can see the hood recesses where the faux trim panels had resided on the previous year's model.

The convertible remained more popular than the coupe body style for 1964.

Hood trim panels, including simulated air vents added the year before, were removed from the 1964 models, but the recesses remained. Convertibles remained the predominant body style with production growing to 13,925 units. Rocker panel trim was simplified as were wheel covers. Steering wheels were walnut-grained plastic, and the variety of colors available for leather seats increased.

Price: $4,037

Engines: 327-ci 250-/300-/365-horsepower V-8 or 327-ci 375-horsepower V-8 (fuel injected)

Transmissions: Three-speed manual, four-speed manual syncromesh, two-speed Powerglide automatic

Total production: 22,229 (13,925 convertibles)

Fact: The convertible body style was still the predominant favorite over the coupe, with ragtops outselling the coupes by more than 5,000 units.

The interior remained basically unchanged, except for more upholstery color choices and the walnut-grained plastic steering wheel as standard equipment.

"Sting Ray" appeared as two words only on the Mid-Years. When the name reappeared in 1969, it was resurrected as a single word.

The basic coupe and convertible body styles remained the same with only minor changes throughout the five years of the Mid-Year models, as seen with this typical 1965 coupe example.

Again, only minor styling changes were made to 1965's models. Side front-fender louvers were changed from horizontal faux units to functional, vertical slots; wheel covers and rocker panel moldings were given even cleaner lines; the hood recesses were removed; and horizontal grille bars were painted black, while outer trim rings remained dressed with chrome.

The real news was under the hood where Chevrolet's big-block engines entered the scene. The 396-ci Turbo Jet V-8, rated at 425 horsepower, created a special bulge in the hood, and it also marked the end of the temperamental small-block fuel-injection systems that had been around since 1957. Four-wheel disc brakes became standard, but buyers could choose drum brakes while supplies lasted.

A steel roll bar was integrated into the fiberglass roof of the Mid-Year coupes; convertible models did not have this added crash protection, which also contributed to structural rigidity for the body.

Price: $4,321

Engines: 327-ci 250-/300-/365-horsepower V-8 or 327-ci 375-horsepower V-8 (fuel injected); 396-ci 425-horsepower V-8

Transmissions: Three-speed manual, four-speed manual syncromesh, two-speed Powerglide automatic

Total production: 23,562 (8,186 coupes)

Fact: Fuel injection was last offered for 1965 and would not reappear on Corvette engines again until 1982 with the introduction of Cross-Fire injection.

The teakwood steering wheel was a classy, if somewhat pricey ($48.45), option. The original radio hang tag is still on the tuning knob of this '65's radio.

The convertible shared all of the sinewy lines of the coupe, making the Mid-Years favorites among collectors.

The convertible remained the more popular of the two body styles, outselling the coupe by almost a 2-to-1 margin. And while the 427-ci engine was developed first, it was the 396-ci big-block that went into the Corvette in 1965, due to a GM policy restricting Corvettes to less than 400 cubic inches. This was also the first major tire size change for the Corvette, with the size changing from 6.70x15 to 7.75x15.

Other popular options introduced in 1965 included side-mount exhausts, gold-wall nylon-cord tires, telescoping steering columns, and teakwood steering wheels.

Price: $4,106

Engines: 327-ci 250-/300-/365-horsepower V-8 or 327-ci 375-horsepower V-8 (fuel injected); 396-ci 425-horsepower V-8

Transmissions: Three-speed manual, four-speed manual syncromesh, two-speed Powerglide automatic

Total production: 23,562 (15,376 convertibles)

Fact: Nineteen sixty-five was the first year the Corvette had two separate hoods: the standard hood for the small-block models, and the big-block hood had a power bulge.

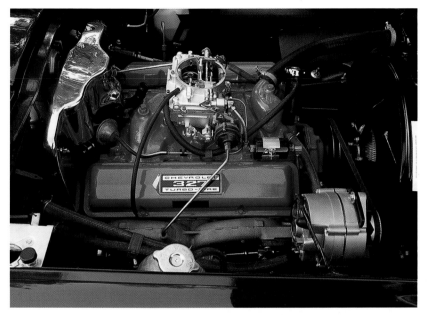

The 327-ci small-block engine was the standard Corvette bill of fare, although it was available in several power output models.

The hideaway headlights that first appeared in 1963 rotated into position when in use and became a Corvette trademark until exposed headlights reappeared on the 2005 model.

The bulging power hood denoted a big-block engine lurking underneath it on 1966 Corvettes.

For 1966, trim alterations included a stylized, elongated "Corvette" script on the hood and revised rocker panel moldings. A new, plated square-mesh egg-crate grille replaced the horizontal bars, and the roof vents were eliminated. It was also the last year knock-off wheels were available.

Backup lights became standard equipment and were built into the existing rear inboard taillight housings, whereas hazard lights were optional.

A 427-ci engine was introduced, and output was initially listed at 450 horsepower but rated downward to 425 horsepower shortly thereafter, ostensibly for insurance purposes.

Price: $4,295

Engines: 327-ci 250-/350-horsepower V-8, 427-ci/390-horsepower V-8, 427-ci/425-horsepower V-8

Transmissions: Three-speed manual, four-speed manual syncromesh, four-speed manual close ratio, four-speed manual heavy-duty close ratio, two-speed Powerglide automatic

Total production: 27,720 (9,958 coupes)

Fact: The 1966 Corvette was not eligible for the SCCA Trans-Am Championship series, due to the upper limit of 5.0 liters on engine displacement. Chevy's only eligible car was the Corvair.

The fender badges also announced to the world that this was a big-block Corvette not to be taken lightly.

The teakwood steering wheel really added a touch of class. Reproduction teakwood wheels for vintage Corvettes now sell for $600–700.

In 1966, ragtops outsold coupes by an almost 2:1 margin; apparently, a lot of buyers enjoyed the feeling of wind in their hair.

Convertibles again proved to be almost twice as popular with the buying public as the coupe model, with almost 18,000 of them rolling off the assembly line, many equipped with the powerful big-block engines. Inside, leather seats were endowed with more pleats to distribute weight better in an effort to reduce split seams, and headrests and shoulder harnesses were also added as options.

Sales volume topped 27,700 units, the highest in Corvette's history to that time.

Price: $4,084

Engines: 327-ci 250-/350-horsepower V-8, 427-ci/390-horsepower V-8, 427-ci/425-horsepower V-8

Transmissions: Three-speed manual, four-speed manual syncromesh, four-speed manual close ratio, four-speed manual heavy-duty close ratio, two-speed Powerglide automatic

Total production: 27,720 (17,762 convertibles)

Fact: Only 37 1966 Corvettes were ordered with the newly available shoulder-harness factory option.

The dual-cowl dash arrangement grouped all of the instruments right in front of the driver and made a roomy glove box possible on the passenger side.

The chrome cover adjacent to the firewall conceals the distributor and provides shielding. Since Corvette bodies were made of fiberglass, radio interference caused by the engine's ignition circuit was a problem unless the coil and distributor were shielded.

The stinger hood and optional side exhausts of big-block '67 Corvettes make them prized and highly coveted among collectors.

Nineteen sixty-seven was supposed to introduce the next-generation (C3) Corvette, but design and production problems delayed it for another year.

Exterior adornments were minimized with much of the trim removed. The hood bulge of the big-block engine was replaced with a stinger scoop. This stinger was emblazoned with the numbers "4-2-7" on each side, disclosing the displacement of the powerplant residing just under it. The stinger hood, in later years, was to become almost legendary as a distinctive feature of what many regarded to be the ultimate Corvette—the 1967 big-block bad boy. In 1967, the heyday of the muscle car era, many law enforcement agencies, including the New Jersey State Troopers, utilized unmarked 427 Corvettes to catch speeders. It was ironic that this massively powered Corvette was the swan song of the Mid-Year era.

The author is the third owner of this unrestored, big-block, 427-ci 390-horsepower 1967 Marlboro Maroon coupe. *Tom Benford*

Price: $4,388.75

Engines: 327-ci 250-/350-horsepower V-8, 427-ci/390-horsepower V-8, 427-ci 400-/435-horsepower V-8; 427-ci 435-horsepower (aluminum cylinder heads, only 16 produced)

Transmissions: Three-speed manual, four-speed manual, four-speed manual close ratio, four-speed manual heavy-duty close ratio, two-speed Powerglide automatic

Total production: 23,940 (8,504 coupes)

Fact: A limited number (20) of L88-option Corvettes, rated at 430 horsepower, were built. This expensive option was aimed primarily at the competitive racing community. Surviving authentic L88s command astronomical prices among collectors.

This car was extremely low-optioned, being factory equipped with shoulder harnesses, transistorized ignition, close-ratio four-speed manual trans, and the monaural AM/FM radio, since it was ordered for a Chevrolet employee who only used it for road racing. The author added side exhausts, bolt-on turbine wheels, air conditioning, and a stereo radio with cassette and a 12-disc CD changer, and had the engine rebuilt (0.60 overbore to displace 439 cubic inches). The paint, chrome, and interior are otherwise all original. *Tom Benford*

The side fender vents, or "gills," increased to five in number, replacing the three larger vents of the preceding year. Options included side-mounted exhausts, cast-aluminum wheels, aluminum cylinder heads, and transistorized ignition; slotted steel rally wheels replaced elaborate wheel covers. Inside, the seats were redesigned and the parking brake handle moved from under the dash to between the seats. Other firsts included four-way flashers, turn signals with a lane-change feature, folding seatback latches, and dual master cylinders.

Meanwhile, the American motoring public anxiously waited for the 1968 rollout of the next-generation Corvette.

The triangular air cleaner denotes the tri-power engine option (three two-barrel carburetors) available on certain 425- and 435-horsepower big-block engines in 1967.

Price: $4,240.75

Engines: 327-ci 250-/350-horsepower V-8, 427-ci/390-horsepower V-8, 427-ci 400-/435-horsepower V-8; 427-ci 435-horsepower (aluminum cylinder heads, only 16 produced)

Transmissions: Three-speed manual, four-speed manual, four-speed manual close ratio, four-speed manual heavy-duty close ratio, two-speed Powerglide automatic

Total production: 23,940 (14,436 convertibles)

Fact: In late February/early March of 1967, some small-blocks received the big-block hood due to a manufacturing problem with the small-block hood mold. However, these were not given the distinctive hood stripe or the engine displacement numerals.

The slotted rally wheels with chrome trim rings and center caps dressed up the rolling gear and gave the Corvette a sporty look.

Aside from redesigned seats and the relocation of the parking brake handle between the seats, the 1967 interior remained basically unchanged.

1968–1982

Chapter 3

Nineteen sixty-eight ushered in the third generation of Corvettes, known as the "Sharks," since their body style derived directly from Bill Mitchell's Mako Shark II show car. The new body shape was described as a "Coke bottle," since it narrowed in the middle at the passenger compartment and widened at both the front and rear of the car. Overall, the 1968s were 7 inches longer and 2 inches lower in height than the previous model, giving them a bold, sleek, lusty appearance. The convertible was still available, but the coupe model now sported removable roof panels. The new car was simply called "Corvette," thus dropping the Sting Ray moniker. Despite initial criticism in the automotive press, the public embraced the 1968 and new sales records were set. Although in 1969 subtle changes occurred, such as moving the ignition switch from the dash to the steering column and adding a map pocket to the dash panel, the body style remained basically the same. The Stingray trademark reappeared, but as one word this time. Small-block engine displacement increased to 350 ci from 327 ci,

and wheel width increased from 7 to 8 inches for better stability. The 250,000th Corvette was produced late in 1969.

Only minor changes were made to the interior and exterior of the 1970 and 1971 models. The Corvette, along with the entire American automotive industry, felt the impact of the OPEC oil embargo. As a result, attention shifted from subtle style changes to engine modifications. In anticipation of Clean Air Act regulations, GM mandated that all its cars would be designed to run on lead-free gasoline with no more than a 91-octane rating. In 1973, a new body-colored urethane front bumper appeared, although chrome was still used on the rear bumper. In 1974, the urethane bumpers appeared on both the front and rear of the car; chrome was never again used on Corvette bumpers.

The 1974–1982 models saw minor styling changes, while emphasis on lower emissions and better fuel economy put serious curbs on the Corvette's performance. During this period, the guard changed at GM. In January 1975, Zora Arkus-Duntov officially resigned

from Chevrolet, and David McLellan took over as chief engineer. Bill Mitchell resigned in 1977, handing the styling reins over to Jerry Palmer and his Chevy 3 Studio staff. And Corvette production began in the new Bowling Green, Kentucky, plant in June 1981, while the last Corvette rolled off the St. Louis assembly line in August (this was the only time in Corvette history that the cars were simultaneously produced in two different plants).

Nineteen eighty-two was the last year of the C3s, the third generation of Corvettes.

Nineteen sixty-eight ushered in the third generation of Corvettes, known as the C3 or Shark era. This was the result of a long-awaited evolution in Corvette design that was ultimately the end product of the experimenting, improving, testing, and tweaking that took place during the previous 15 years of Corvette development.

As the story goes, Bill Mitchell, GM's styling chief, went deep-sea fishing in the Bahamas and, upon landing a shark, dreamed up a new body shape for the Corvette. Mitchell's dream culminated in the Larry Shinoda–designed Mako Shark II test/show car unveiled at the New York International Auto Show and the General Motors Pavilion at the World's Fair in 1965.

The coupe featured two removable T-top panels, with a bar separating the two to give the body added rigidity.

Price: $4,663

Engines: 327-ci 300-/350-horsepower V-8, 427-ci/390-horsepower V-8, 427-ci 400-/435-horsepower V-8; 427-ci 430-horsepower V-8 (aluminum cylinder heads, only 80 produced)

Transmissions: Three-speed manual, four-speed manual, four-speed manual close ratio, four-speed manual heavy-duty close ratio, three-speed Turbo Hydra-matic automatic

Total production: 28,566 (9,936 coupes)

Fact: Pontiac almost beat Chevrolet to the Coke-bottle-design body with its 1965 Banshee, a two-seat convertible sports car that would have been in competition with the Corvette, which is why GM stopped it.

Due to the Coke-bottle body shape that narrowed in the middle, interior room in the Sharks was considerably less than it had been in previous Corvette models.

Simply called "Corvette" in 1968, the Sting Ray moniker had been dropped.

Unofficially dubbed the "Shark," the 1968 Corvette had clean, aerodynamic lines. The boat-tail rear deck, humped fenders, and sleek hood of the Sting Rays were gone, replaced by a long pointed nose, bulges over the wheels, a pinched midsection, and a concave, notch-backed rear deck. The coupes had sail panels flanking an upright, removable flat rear window and removable two-panel T-roofs. Four gills added to the fenders helped reduce underhood air pressure. The '68s were 7 inches longer and 2 inches lower in height than Mid-Years.

Other innovations included vacuum-operated headlights that popped up rather than rotating into position as with the Mid-Years. Side vent windows were eliminated, windshield

This 1968 convertible has an optional vinyl-covered auxiliary hardtop. The vinyl covering added an additional $52.70 to the hardtop's base price of $231.75.

wipers hid under a vacuum-operated panel, and the battery was relocated behind the driver seat. A three-speed Turbo Hydra-matic transmission replaced the two-speed Powerglide, and aluminum heads on the 427-ci engine were optional. In one test, a 427-equipped coupe did 0 to 60 in 5.7 seconds and a quarter-mile in 14.1 seconds.

Even with initial trade media criticism, the new Shark was a hit with the public—so much so that new Corvette sales records were set.

Split rear bumpers and two-on-a-side taillights were design carryovers from the Mid-Years. The side marker lights, however, were a new addition.

Price: $4,320

Engines: 327-ci 300-/350-horsepower V-8, 427-ci/390-horsepower V-8, 427-ci 400-/435-horsepower V-8; 427-ci 430-horsepower V-8 (aluminum cylinder heads, only 80 produced)

Transmissions: Three-speed manual, four-speed manual, four-speed manual close ratio, four-speed manual heavy-duty close ratio, three-speed Turbo Hydra-matic automatic

Total production: 28,566 (18,630 convertibles)

Fact: For 1968, a factory-installed antitheft alarm system was offered as an option, but fewer than 400 cars were ordered with it.

Flush door handles added to the sleekness of the new Shark.

Side exhausts with chromed covers were a popular option, especially on big-block '69 Sharks.

While the 1969 Corvette was almost identical to its immediate predecessor, a number of complaints about the 1968 were corrected in the new edition. The steering wheel was trimmed an inch for greater driver entry and egress, door panels were redesigned for increased shoulder room, the ignition switch moved to the steering column, map pockets were installed in the instrument panel, and optional side exhausts were available.

Price: $4,781

Engines: 350-ci 300-/350-horsepower V-8, 427-ci 390-/400-/430-/435-horsepower V-8; 427-ci 430-horsepower V-8 (special L88/ZL-1, only two produced)

Transmissions: Three-speed manual, four-speed manual, four-speed manual close ratio, four-speed manual heavy-duty close ratio, three-speed Turbo Hydra-matic automatic

Total production: 38,762 (22,129)

Fact: The 250,000th Corvette was produced late in the year.

With the T-tops removed, driving or riding in the Corvette coupe was almost like being in a convertible model.

The big-block engines with tri-power (three two-barrel carburetors) were favorites with the speed- and power-hungry buyers.

The license plate tells you there's a tri-power big-block under the hood of this bad-boy '69 Shark ragtop.

The Stingray trademark reappeared in 1969, as a single word this time. Small-block engine displacement increased to 350 ci from 327 ci, and wheel width increased from 7 to 8 inches for better stability.

Even with a strike closing the assembly line early in the year, total production saw 22,129 coupes and 16,633 convertibles come off the line; this was the first year that coupes outnumbered convertibles. The total 38,762 production yield wouldn't be matched again until 1976.

Price: $4,438

Engines: 350-ci 300-/350-horsepower V-8, 427-ci 390-/400-/430-/435-horsepower V-8; 427-ci 430-horsepower V-8 (special L88/ZL-1, only two produced)

Transmissions: Three-speed manual, four-speed manual, four-speed manual close ratio, four-speed manual heavy-duty close ratio, three-speed Turbo Hydra-matic automatic

Total production: 38,762 (16,633 convertibles)

Fact: In 1969, the ignition switch was moved from the dash to the steering column, where it would remain until 1997, when it returned back to the dash.

The optional side exhausts with chrome covers really give the profile of this 1969 Corvette some extra eye appeal.

The hood bulge, side exhausts, chrome fender gill trim, and low, sloping nose make this '69 Shark look fast even standing still.

The coupes continued to be more popular than the convertibles in 1970, and with the T-tops removed, you had the best of both worlds.

For 1970, the fenders were flared to reduce wheel-thrown debris, a problem with the 1968 and 1969 models. The grille evolved from horizontal bars into an egg-crate pattern used for fender louvers that replaced the four gills of the two preceding years. Front parking lights were rectangular rather than round, and the dual exhaust outlets were squared off.

Price: $5,192

Engines: 350-ci 300-/350-/370-horsepower V-8; 454-ci 390-horsepower V-8

Transmissions: Three-speed manual, four-speed manual, four-speed manual close ratio, four-speed manual heavy-duty close ratio, three-speed Turbo Hydra-matic automatic

Total production: 17,316 (10,668 coupes)

Fact: 1970 sales were their lowest since 1962 due to a late start in the production year.

"Stingray" side script adorned the front fenders right above the egg-crate fender gills.

The small-block Chevy engine, now displacing 350 ci (up from 327 ci), was the standard power-plant for the 1970 Corvette, and it was more than adequate for providing plenty of get-up and go.

The most noticeable styling change was the egg-crate grille that replaced the gills behind the wheelwells.

Subtle interior refinements included redesigned seats for more headroom, and easier access was provided to the rear storage compartment. Optional luxuries included custom interiors with leather seat trim, wood-grain accents, lower carpet trim on door panels, wood-grain console accents, and cut-pile carpeting.

The original high-performance LT-1 engine, a small-block 350-ci powerplant with solid lifters producing 370 horsepower, was introduced. Big-block displacement grew to 454 ci, rated at 390 horsepower in the LS5 model.

Price: $4,849

Engines: 350-ci 300-/350-/370-horsepower V-8; 454-ci 390-horsepower V-8

Transmissions: Three-speed manual, four-speed manual, four-speed manual close ratio, four-speed manual heavy-duty close ratio, three-speed Turbo Hydra-matic automatic

Total production: 17,316 (6,648 convertibles)

Fact: In 1970, displacement for the big-block engines increased from 427 to 454 ci and the powerful 370-hp LT1 small-block engine debuted.

The interior, despite efforts to increase room, remained cramped compared to the roominess of C1s and Mid-Years.

For some folks, it just wasn't a real Corvette unless it was a convertible, attested to by the fact that 6,648 buyers opted for the ragtop model in 1970.

The deep-dish slotted-steel rally wheels with chrome trim rings and center caps gave the Corvette an aggressive, no-nonsense stance.

America was soon to feel the impact of the OPEC oil embargo, and federally mandated emissions restrictions put a dampener on the demand for horsepower and speed. As a result, attention to engine modifications became the big issue with Corvettes. Compression ratios were lowered to accommodate lower-octane and unleaded fuels.

Price: $5,496 (coupe), $5,259 (convertible)

Engines: 350-ci 270-/330-horsepower V-8; 454-ci 365-/425-horsepower V-8

Transmissions: Three-speed manual, four-speed manual close ratio, four-speed manual heavy-duty close ratio, Turbo Hydra-matic

Total production: 21,811 (14,680 coupes, 7,121 convertibles)

Fact: A special big-block, 454-ci, 425-horsepower V-8 engine with aluminum heads was available as an option that ran on low-lead fuel and could be used with an automatic transmission.

Though the days of the big-block engine were starting to dwindle, it remained the powerplant of choice for the true power junkies.

Though side trim was sparse, the egg-crate fender grille served to spice things up a bit.

This was the last year that the egg-crate side fender grille and front chrome bumpers would be seen on the Corvette.

The LT-1 option gave the speed-and-power seekers the extra ponies they desired.

The close-ratio four-speed manual gearbox was selected by 3,494 buyers.

Nineteen seventy-two was the last year for side fender and front egg-crate grilles and the removable rear window, as well as chrome bumpers on the front and rear of the car. Alarm systems, which were optional in earlier model years, became standard.

Price: $5,533 (coupe), $5,296 (convertible)

Engines: 350-ci 200-/255-horsepower V-8; 454-ci 270-horsepower V-8

Transmissions: Three-speed manual, four-speed manual close ratio, Turbo Hydra-matic

Total production: 27,004 (20,495 coupes, 6,508 convertibles)

Fact: This was the first year air conditioning could be combined with the LT-1 engine. Prior to 1972, the increased rpm of the high-performance engine ran the risk of air conditioning belts being spun off.

Aftermarket accessory chrome luggage carriers mounted to the rear deck were a remedy for the severe lack of storage space in Sharks.

For 1973, the front hood was extended rearward over the windshield wipers, eliminating the vacuum-operated lift panels that were used between 1968 and 1972 to conceal wiper mechanisms. Metal side-impact beams were incorporated into the inside of doors, per federal mandate. Since the rear windows were no longer removable, luggage space increased 2 inches because of the removal of the window's storage shelf.

Price: $5,561

Engines: 350-ci 190-/250-horsepower V-8; 454-ci 275-horsepower V-8

Transmissions: Three-speed manual, four-speed manual close ratio, Turbo Hydra-matic

Total production: 30,464 (25,521 coupes)

Fact: The departure of chrome front bumpers allowed the installation of body-color front end systems that met federal 5-mile-per-hour impact requirements; however, the new package added 35 pounds.

While Corvettes still used the hideaway headlight scheme that debuted in 1963, the headlights popped open and shut rather than rotating into and out of position, as they had with the Mid-Years.

The egg-crate gills were gone for 1973, now replaced with a single miniature cove on the front fenders.

The popularity of the convertible was definitely waning, as the coupe version outsold it by a five-to-one ratio in 1973.

Aluminum wheels were once again listed as an option in 1973. However, their inability to maintain air pressure (reminiscent of the problems that plagued the early 1963 aluminum knock-off wheels), kept them out of the hands of customers until 1976. And for the first time, radial tires were used.

Price: $5,398

Engines: 350-ci 190-/250-horsepower V-8; 454-ci 275-horsepower V-8

Transmissions: Three-speed manual, four-speed manual close ratio, Turbo Hydra-matic

Total production: 30,464 (4,943 convertibles)

Fact: The body-colored front bumper was made of urethane, which ultimately proved to be very susceptible to UV rays and, over a period of time, developed cracks and deteriorated.

The big-block engine, though only outputting 275 horsepower, was still the chosen option for 4,412 buyers.

The optional Turbo Hydra-matic automatic trans was popular with those who didn't want to go through the gears manually.

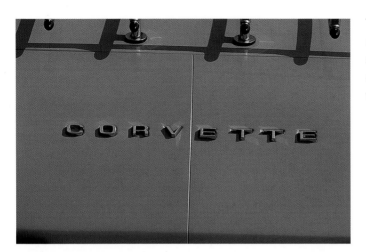

The molding process for the urethane rear bumper had some problems to be worked out, so a two-piece bumper was used, but only for 1974.

The vents behind the removable rear window were for the Astro-Ventilation system that circulated fresh air within the cabin area; in truth, it didn't work all that well.

With the chrome bumpers replaced by body-colored units, exterior bright work was minimal on the 1974 Shark.

The days of cheap and plentiful gas supplies were waning, as the Arab oil embargo, declared in late 1973, was felt at the gas pump. And soaring insurance rates for high-powered models were making consumers think twice. As a result, 1974 was the last model year for which the big-block engine was available and also the last year without catalytic converters to control emissions. Future engines would run on unleaded gas, and dual exhausts would be replaced by manifolds connected to the converters.

Price: $6,001.50

Engines: 350-ci 195-/250-horsepower V-8; 454-ci 275-horsepower V-8

Transmissions: Three-speed manual, four-speed manual close ratio, three-speed Turbo Hydra-matic

Total production: 37,502 (32,028 coupes)

Fact: Nineteen seventy-four was the last year the Corvette was produced to run on leaded gasoline.

The transition to impact-absorbing body-color bumpers was complete with the urethane skin covering an aluminum impact bar on two telescoping brackets. Nineteen seventy-four Corvettes are distinguished by a vertical split in their rear bumpers, a feature unique to that model year.

Radiators were reworked to provide better cooling at low speeds. The inside rearview mirror was widened to 10 inches, and shoulder safety straps were added to lap belts.

Convertible production continued to shrink, and coupes outnumbered them by a ratio of nearly 6 to 1. The coupe's price tag broke the $6,000 barrier by $1.50.

The body-colored urethane front and rear bumpers gave the 1974 Shark a somewhat lackluster appearance almost totally devoid of chrome.

Price: $5,765.50

Engines: 350-ci 195-/250-horsepower V-8; 454-ci 275-horsepower V-8

Transmissions: Three-speed manual, four-speed manual close ratio, three-speed Turbo Hydra-matic

Total production: 37,502 (5,474 convertibles)

Fact: The rearview mirror in the 1974 Corvette was increased to a width of 10 inches.

The engine bay became ever more cramped for space as additional air-pollution plumbing was added, especially with this, the last year of the big-block motor.

If you look closely you can see the seam joining the left and right halves of the urethane rear bumper. Once the engineers got the molding problems sorted out, a one-piece rear bumper was used on subsequent years.

This optional vinyl covering for the auxiliary hardtop was ordered by 279 convertible buyers.

This was the last year ragtops were available until resurrected in 1986. High Energy Ignition (HEI), Corvette's first no-points distributor, made its first appearance. It required that the tachometer be driven electronically instead of mechanically, and speedometers were also calibrated in kilometers per hour for the first time in addition to standard miles per hour readings.

Price: $6,810.10 (coupe); $6,550.10 (convertible)

Engines: 350-ci 165-/205-horsepower V-8

Transmissions: Three-speed manual, four-speed manual close ratio, Turbo Hydra-matic

Total production: 38,465 (33,836 coupes, 4,639 convertibles)

Fact: This was the first year for headlight warning buzzers.

Only small-block 350-ci engines were offered, with 165 horsepower standard and a 205-horsepower version as an option.

The urethane rear bumper became a sloping, one-piece unit for 1975.

The nose of the car tilts forward for engine access, a feature not seen on production Corvettes until the C4s debuted in 1984. The exaggerated fender flares, front and rear spoilers, and top fender gills required lots of fiberglass work. Twenty-four coats of custom-mixed pearl paint were used to achieve the stunning silver-to-blue fade effect. *Tom Benford*

The convertible had disappeared, but 46,558 people opted for a 1976 basic Corvette sport coupe of their own. An in-glass rear window defogger replaced forced hot air, and GM's freedom battery—a new sealed, maintenance-free unit—was included in all models.

Price: $7,604.85 coupe only

Engines: 350-ci 180-/210-horsepower V-8

Transmissions: Three-speed manual, four-speed close-ratio manual, Turbo Hydra-matic

Total production: 46,558

Fact: A new sport steering wheel, adapted from the Chevrolet Vega, was added, much to the dismay of many Corvette fans.

The '76 custom has its own stylized logo airbrushed into the coves on both sides of the car. *Tom Benford*

The fenders had to be flared at all four corners to accommodate the extra-wide custom-made wire wheels and tires. *Tom Benford*

For 1977, vinyl seats were out and leather was standard, although cloth seats with leather trim were available at no extra cost. This was also the last year for the vertical rear window.

A new column, which moved the steering wheel several inches closer to the instrument panel, permitted easier entry and exit and a more comfortable driving position; it also housed the headlight controls and the windshield wiper/washer switch.

The Stingray trade name disappeared and was replaced by the crossed-flags logo.

This was the last year for the vertical rear window, which had been around since the first Shark appeared in 1968.

Price: $8,647 (coupe only)

Engines: 350-ci 180-/210-horsepower V-8

Transmissions: Three-speed manual, four-speed manual close ratio, three-speed Turbo Hydra-matic

Total production: 49,213

Fact: The 500,000th Corvette was driven off the assembly line early in the year.

From the outside, the 1977 Corvette was nearly a dead ringer for its predecessor.

The round quad taillights that began with the Mid-Year models remained a Corvette trademark.

The 1978 Corvette featured the first major restyling since the Shark era began in 1968.

The Corvette reached its silver anniversary, and it was declared the pace car for that year's Indianapolis 500 race. Chevrolet offered two commemorative packages: a special Silver Anniversary paint scheme and replica models of the Indy pace car selling for an unprecedented $13,653.

Price: $9,351.89 (25th Anniversary coupe)

Engines: 350-ci 175-/185-/220-horsepower V-8

Transmissions: Three-speed manual, four-speed manual close ratio, three-speed Turbo Hydra-matic

Total production: 40,274 (includes 15,283 with Silver Anniversary paint scheme but excludes pace car replica editions)

Fact: Twenty-fifth anniversary logos were used on the front and rear exclusively on all 1978 Corvettes.

In addition to increasing rear storage space, the instrument panel received a major facelift for 1978.

All 1978 Corvettes were adorned with the special Silver Anniversary badges.

The pace car replicas—all 6,502 of them—were popular with buyers in 1978.

An extensive redesign featured a new fastback rear end (a look that would last five years) with a large rear window that increased storage space considerably. This was the first fastback rear window on a Corvette since 1967.

Other changes included a squared-off speedometer and tachometer, a larger 24-gallon gas tank, a reworked antitheft system that included the T-tops, and inner door panels with screw-in armrests rather than the molded-in style prevalent since 1965.

Price: $13,653.21 (pace car replica edition)

Engines: 350-ci 175-/185-/220-horsepower V-8

Transmissions: Three-speed manual, four-speed manual close ratio, three-speed Turbo Hydra-matic

Total production: 6,502 (excludes basic and special paint 25th Anniversary editions)

Fact: The 1978 pace car's distinguishing black-and-silver paint was chosen over other alternative color schemes primarily because it photographed well; back then, most magazine articles and ads were still done in black and white rather than color.

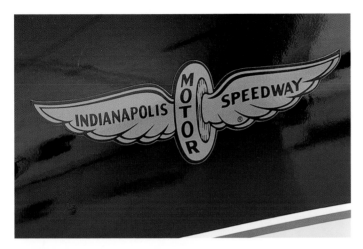

"Indy" decals and other special ornamentation identified the pace car replicas.

The Corvette engine bay became a very crowded place indeed, thanks to the smog pump and extra plumbing necessitated by stringently enforced emissions restrictions.

"Limited Edition" was a misnomer for the pace car replicas. They were produced in such huge numbers (over 6,500 of them) that they were commonplace rather than the rare collector models some buyers hoped they would be.

The 1979 profile looked low and sleek, accented by the sloping rear window.

Several popular features from the Silver Anniversary editions were carried over into 1979 models, including the high seatback design, which became standard equipment, as did an AM/FM radio.

Outside front and rear air spoilers were available as options, and tungsten-halogen headlights replaced high-beam units for increased visibility.

Modifications to muffler design and air intake permitted minor horsepower improvements to the basic 350-ci engine. Sticker price for the basic coupe exceeded $10,000 for the first time.

The 1979 model was the high-water mark in Corvette production. There were 53,807 coupes made available to the motoring public, a record that still stands.

There were no major interior changes for 1979.

The front and rear spoilers were popular options.

Price: $10,220

Engines: 350-ci 175-/225-horsepower V-8

Transmissions: Three-speed manual, four-speed manual close ratio, three-speed Turbo Hydra-matic

Total production: 53,807

Fact: Nineteen seventy-nine was a record-setting year for Corvette production, with over 53,800 units manufactured.

Federal mandates impacted performance and had a substantial impact on sales for 1980.

The Turbo Hydra-matic transmission option was popular, as real Corvette performance had become a nonevent due to the low horsepower output caused by strict emissions regulations.

Federal and state mandates for increased fuel efficiency and reduced pollution impacted the Corvette. For the first time since 1974, two engine displacements were available: the standard 350-ci and a 305-ci required for the California market where emissions regulations were more stringent. The 305, only available for that one year, was a standard Chevrolet passenger car engine that was only available with automatic transmissions. Weight-trimming measures included lower density roof panels, thinner hood and outer door thicknesses, and aluminum in the differential housing and cross-member; aluminum intake manifolds also became standard. Government-mandated restrictions brought sales down by more than 13,000 units from the previous year, while the base sticker price rose more than $3,000.

Although the appearance didn't change much, lighter, weight-saving materials were used both inside and out in 1980 to increase fuel efficiency.

Price: $13,140.24

Engines: 350-ci 175-/230-horsepower V-8; 305-ci 180-horsepower V-8 (California)

Transmissions: Three-speed manual, four-speed manual close ratio, three-speed Turbo Hydra-matic

Total production: 40,614

Fact: Speedometers were limited to an 85-mile-per-hour maximum due to federal mandates.

Again, the appearance of the Corvette remained basically unchanged for 1981.

As the year began, Corvettes were being built in both St. Louis and a new facility in Bowling Green, Kentucky. The first Kentucky-built unit rolled off the line in June, while St. Louis manufacture was phased out in August. St. Louis–built units were mostly solid color cars using traditional lacquers, while Bowling Green–built two-tone units used a new enamel-type paint with clear-coat finishes.

No engine options were offered in 1981 since the 350-ci block was now California-certified and available throughout the United States with both four-speed manual and automatic transmissions. Chevrolet's computer command control, which automatically adjusted engine timing and air/fuel mixture, became standard equipment on all models.

Weight reduction remained a key design factor. A fiberglass monoleaf rear spring weighing only 8 pounds was introduced, and all 1981 valve covers were made of lightweight magnesium.

There was nothing to write home and tell the folks about under the hood, either, as there were no engine options available for 1981.

Judging by its solid-white exterior, chances are pretty good that this 1981 Corvette is wearing lacquer paint put on at the St. Louis factory. Two-tone 1981 models used base-coat/clear-coat finishes and were built in Bowling Green, Kentucky.

Price: $16,258.52

Engines: 350-ci 185-horsepower V-8

Transmissions: Three-speed manual, four-speed manual, Turbo Hydra-matic

Total production: 40,606 (8,995 were built in Bowling Green)

Fact: The antitheft alarm system had an ignition interrupt added to prevent engine startup.

The two-tone paint that divided at the beltline made up for the lack of brightwork on the Collector Editions.

The 1982 model was the last year of the Shark era. Everything that could be done had been done to increase the cramped interior space for both driver and passenger, but it was still far from what anyone could call roomy.

As the Corvette's third era was drawing to a close, power and fuel economy were improved with Cross-Fire injection: two injectors were mated to the computer command control system capable of making 80 adjustments per second. The exhaust system was redesigned with smaller and lighter catalytic converters, and the exhaust pipes entering the converter were reworked to allow hotter exhaust gases and thus boost efficiency. Hoods had solenoid-operated doors that ushered fresh air directly to the air filter during full-throttle operation, which helped to give a slight power boost.

The deep-dish slotted aluminum wheels worked well with the silver/black color scheme and gave it some additional continuity.

Price: $18,290.07

Engines: 350-ci 200-horsepower V-8

Transmissions: Turbo Hydra-matic only

Total production: 18,648 (excludes Collector Editions)

Fact: For the first time since 1955, a standard transmission was not available.

The 1982 Corvette was the last of the Shark era and ended the third generation for the marque.

To mark the phasing out of the Shark series, a special Collector Edition was offered. Nineteen eighty-two was also the first year the Corvette sold for over $20,000—$22,537.59 to be exact.

Price: $22,537.59

Engines: 350-ci 200-horsepower V-8

Transmissions: Turbo Hydra-matic only

Total production: 6,759 (excludes standard coupes)

Fact: In 1982, fuel injection reappeared in the Corvette after a 17-year hiatus.

The 1982 Collector Edition option commemorated the end of the C3 generation with special emblems.

The new Cross-Fire injection system heralded the return of performance engineering for the Corvette.

The lifting hatchback rear window made accessing the storage area considerably easier and more functional, but it was only available on the Collector Edition for 1982.

1984–1996

Chapter 4

In 1984, the new fourth-generation Corvette, also known as the C4, made its debut. The new car had a wider, smoother, aerodynamic body style, more spacious interior, lightweight chassis, integral stability, and even further weight reduction. It became the first, really all-new Corvette since the 1968 Shark appeared. A new single-unit, removable Targa-type roof replaced the T-tops, and a flip-nose assembly opened forward like a clam shell to permit easier access to the engine compartment.

The Corvette continued to evolve from 1984 through 1996, becoming more civilized and refined with many heretofore optional creature comforts, such as air conditioning, power steering, power seats, high-end stereo systems, and automatic transmissions, becoming standard equipment. In March 1989, Chevrolet introduced the high-performance Corvette ZR-1 at the Geneva Auto Show in Switzerland, and in April, planning began on the new C5 (fifth-generation) Corvette, which would make its debut some eight years later.

In September 1992, Corvette chief engineer Dave McLellan formally retired but stayed on as a consultant until his replacement was named. That November, Dave Hill, an engineer in GM's Cadillac program, accepted the job offer to succeed McLellan as the Corvette's chief engineer.

The Corvette's evolution continued, and its sinewy lines got sleeker. The entire upper portion of the nose tilted forward like a clam shell to provide easier access to the engine bay.

The exterior of the 1985 model was unchanged from the preceding year, but with the numerous innovations introduced in the 1984, there were electrical problems and a rough ride that had to be corrected. The latter was taken care of by adjusting suspension rates as much as 26 percent and using larger stabilizer bars to compensate for spring softness in certain models. True fuel injection, supplied by Bosch, replaced the Cross-Fire injection system and increased horsepower from 205 to 230 while improving fuel efficiency.

The brake master cylinder bore was increased, and the brake booster was made of plastic, making it lighter and more corrosion-resistant—a first in an American car. Manual transmissions, available again, came with a heavier-duty differential, and rear axle gearing was improved.

In one test, the 1985 Corvette did 0–60 miles per hour in 5.7 seconds and the quarter-mile in 14.1 seconds.

The slotted "Cuisinart" wheels derived their nickname from their vectors, which looked like food processor blades.

Price: $24,403

Engines: 350-ci 230-horsepower V-8

Transmissions: Four-speed manual, Turbo Hydra-matic

Total production: 39,729

Fact: With the CB radio craze dwindling, 1985 was the last year a CB radio was offered as an option, and only 16 Corvettes were ordered with one.

The lumpy, rectangular protrusion on the passenger side of the dash was unaffectionately known as the "bread loaf" due to its shape. Its purpose was to provide additional crash padding in anticipation of expected federal safety mandates that never came to pass.

The 1990 Corvette coupe was virtually undistinguishable from the high-power, high-priced ZR-1 version except for a few subtle changes.

While the ZR-1 was the big news for 1990, the standard L98 engine's rating was kicked up 5 horsepower to 245 horsepower thanks to an air-intake speed-density control system, camshaft revision, and increased compression ratio in convertibles. And five additional horsepower (250 horsepower) was achieved in the coupe because of its less-restrictive exhaust system.

All 1990 models were given redesigned hybrid instrument panels combining a digital speedometer with analog tach, as well as secondary gauges and a display that alerted the driver when an oil change was needed based on an engine oil-life monitor. A driver-side air bag was added, and a 200-watt stereo system was available (one unit offering a theft-proof compact disc player).

Price: $31,979 coupe, $37,264 convertible

Engines: 350-ci 245-/250-horsepower V-8;
350-ci 375-horsepower V-8 (ZR-1 only)

Transmissions: Four-speed automatic, six-speed manual

Total production: 23,646 (16,016 coupes,
including 3,049 ZR-1s; 7,630 convertibles)

Fact: The engine oil-life monitor calculated
useful oil life based on temperatures and
revolutions.

The classic, round taillights and the somewhat
concave rear fascia immediately set ordinary
1990 Corvettes apart from their high-powered,
high-priced sibling, the ZR-1s.

The redesigned hybrid dash combined analog and digital instrumentation.

The ZR-1 had a wider tail section with a convex rear fascia; otherwise, it looked like the standard 1990 Corvette.

Price: $58,995

Engines: 350-ci 375-horsepower V-8

Transmissions: Six-speed manual

Total production: 3,049 (coupe only)

Fact: Some dealers asked—and were paid—$100,000 for the then ultimate in American sports cars.

Supple leather wraparound seats imparted both comfort and a real race-car feel for the driver and passenger in the ZR-1.

The slightly squared-off taillights distinguished the ZR-1 from other 1990 Corvettes, which retained round taillights. The ZR-1 emblem at the rear of the car is the view most other drivers got of this awesome beast.

This is what made it the "King of the Hill." The four-cam, 32-valve, LT5 engine had an aluminum block and cranked out an incredible 375 horses.

The King of the Hill had arrived. General Motors and its Corvette division approached Group Lotus in Great Britain to develop the world's fastest production car. This collaboration produced the LT5 engine, an aluminum-block V-8 with the same bore as the standard (L98) 350-ci but capable of 375 horsepower. The new block featured four overhead camshafts and 32 valves. The LT5s were built by Mercury Marine in Oklahoma and assembled into the ZR-1 vehicle at Bowling Green.

A unique computerized engine-control module provided bi-modal characteristics: the ZR-1 could be used for routine street driving or as a race car—with increased speed and handling available on demand. A key-operated valet switch locked out the upper speed ranges, limiting power to a normal 250 horses and thus preventing inexperienced hands from unleashing the car's awesome power. Available only in coupe configuration, the ZR-1 didn't come cheap: the ZR-1 option cost $27,016.

The wraparound light package changed the look of the 1991 Corvette, although the rest of the car looked the same.

With the success of the 1990 ZR-1, all 1991 Corvettes adopted many of its exterior body innovations, including a similar restyled rear with convex fascia and four square taillights. The brake light remained integrated into the rear fascia on convertibles and stayed atop the rear window on coupes. A lower, tapered wraparound nose housed the parking, fog, and directional lights. On the interior, electrical sockets were provided for a cellular phone or other 12-volt devices; a power delay feature permitted the radio/stereo and power windows to be operated for 15 minutes after the ignition was turned off or until the driver's door was opened.

The 1991 ZR-1 was unique, with improved doors and newly designed 11-inch-wide rear wheels. Among the options were heavy-duty suspension components that permitted ride adjustments from firm to very firm, rather than from soft to firm as in earlier systems. The valet switch was retained.

Price: $32,455 coupe, $38,770 convertible

Engines: 350-ci 245-/250-horsepower V-8; 350-ci 375-horsepower V-8 (ZR-1 only)

Transmissions: Four-speed automatic, six-speed manual

Total production: 20,639 (14,967 coupes, including 2,044 ZR-1s; 5,672 convertibles)

Fact: An oil pan float was built into the instrument display to warn of low oil.

The amber digital display combined with the amber-toned numerals of the analog instruments gave the gauge panel a very futuristic look and feel that, at the time, was in vogue.

The 234-horsepower 350-ci engine was standard, while a 250-horsepower version was optional, or, for another $31,683, you could get the 375-horsepower ZR-1 package with additional goodies.

Though exterior changes were few, performance improved with the LT1, the next generation of the small-block engine. While the displacement remained at 350 ci, it was able to produce 300 horsepower at 5,000 rpm. Top speed of the LT1 was rated at 160 miles per hour, and it was capable of achieving 0–60 in 5.7 seconds and the quarter-mile in 14.1 seconds.

Computer-controlled ignition timing, a higher compression ratio, a new camshaft, multiport fuel injection, free-flow cylinder heads, and a low-restriction exhaust system all contributed to the power boost.

Exterior changes were very minimal for 1992, the year the one-millionth Corvette was made.

Price: $33,635 coupe, $40,145 convertible

Engines: 350-ci 300-horsepower V-8; 350-ci 375-horsepower (ZR-1 only)

Transmissions: Four-speed automatic, six-speed manual

Total production: 20,479 (14,604 coupes, 5,875 convertibles)

Fact: The 1,000,000th Corvette, a white convertible, rolled off the assembly line in 1992.

Removing the one-piece roof panel provided the fresh-air freedom of a convertible with the added safety and security of a coupe.

The black powder–coated rear badge and the embossed Corvette name gave the rear a more contemporary look.

With the 1993 Corvette, the marque entered its fourth decade and was truly regarded as an American icon.

To mark the occasion of Corvette entering its fourth decade, a 40th Anniversary edition was offered featuring an exclusive Ruby Red metallic exterior and leather sports seats, special wheel center trim, and emblems in the same special color. Aside from the special anniversary edition, leather seats in all 1993 Corvettes carried a 40th Anniversary emblem on the headrest. Beyond that, exterior styling was virtually unchanged from the 1992 model.

The LT1 engine, introduced a year earlier, was made quieter, thermo-set polyester valve covers replaced the former magnesium units, and the camshaft exhaust lobe profile was modified to help increase torque.

The 1993 Corvette was the first GM product to feature a passive keyless entry (PKE) system. A battery-operated transmitter locked and unlocked doors when the driver approached or departed the vehicle.

The headrests of all 1993 Corvettes bore the 40th Anniversary logo.

Price: $34,595 coupe, $41,195 convertible

Engines: 350-ci 300-horsepower V-8; 350-ci 405-horsepower V-8 (ZR-1 only)

Transmissions: Four-speed automatic, six-speed manual

Total production: 21,590 (15,898 coupes, 5,692 convertibles; includes 6,700 40th Anniversary specials and 448 ZR-1s)

Fact: The ZR-1 option made the Corvette America's most powerful automobile when its LT5 engine received a power boost from 375 to 405 horses.

The leather form-fitting, wraparound seats made driving even long distances comfortable.

From the outside, the 1994 Corvette looked like the 1993 edition.

The exterior remained unchanged from 1993, but multiport fuel injection was replaced by a new sequential fuel-injection system that improved response, drivability, idle, and emissions. Electronic controls in a redesigned standard four-speed automatic transmission improved shift quality, and a safety interlock was incorporated.

Inside, a passenger-side air bag was added, the two-spoke steering wheel with driver's air bag was redesigned, the white instrument panel graphics transformed into a tangerine hue at night, all seats were leather, and individual power seat adjustment controls were relocated to the console. Convertible rear windows were changed from plastic to glass with defrosters/defoggers built into the glass panel. Goodyear Extended Mobility Tires (run-flat), which allowed continued use under zero tire pressure conditions, were optional on some models.

The four-speed automatic transmission was standard on the Corvette for 1994.

Though it looked the same as the earlier editions, the 350-ci engine was fed with sequential fuel injection in 1994.

Price: $36,185 coupe, $42,960 convertible

Engines: 350-ci 300-horsepower V-8; 350-ci 405-horsepower V-8 (ZR-1 only)

Transmissions: Four-speed automatic, six-speed manual

Total production: 23,330 (17,984 coupes, including 448 ZR-1s; 5,346 convertibles)

Fact: The National Corvette Museum opened in Bowling Green, Kentucky, on September 2, 1994.

The 1995 exterior incorporated new front fender gill-style air vents, and, once again, Corvette was chosen as the Indianapolis 500 pace car.

Extended-mobility (run-flat) radial tires, an option on the 1994 platform, eliminated the need for a spare tire, so 1995s could be purchased with weight and wallet savings. A read-out for automatic transmission fluid temperatures was added to the instrument panel, and a better radio mount prevented skipping when compact discs were played.

Redesigned clutch controls in the four-speed automatic transmission provided smoother shifting, and the six-speed manual transmission was reworked for easier operation. The larger brake package, previously found on the ZR-1, was standard, and anti-lock braking and traction control systems were included on all 1995 models.

Again, the exterior of the 1995 Corvette duplicated the look of its predecessors.

Price: $36,785 coupe, $43,665 convertible

Engines: 350-ci 300-horsepower V-8; 350-ci 405-horsepower V-8 (ZR-1 only)

Transmissions: Four-speed automatic, six-speed manual

Total production: 20,742 (15,771 coupes, including 448 ZR-1s; 4,971 convertibles, including 527 pace car replicas)

Fact: This was the last year for the ZR-1, which was still a $31,258 option package. Over its six-year life span, a total of 6,939 ZR-1s were built.

A transmission fluid temperature read-out and better radio mounting to minimize CD skipping comprised the interior changes for 1995.

The 350-ci 300-horsepower engine remained unchanged for 1995.

The second Collector Edition Corvette was offered in 1996, the last year of the C4 generation.

To commemorate the last year of the fourth generation (C4), the company offered another silver Collector Edition and a special, limited-run Grand Sport edition as well.

The Grand Sport was Admiral Blue with a wide white center stripe, and it used five-spoke ZR-1 wheels painted black. Coupes featured rear fender flares to accommodate wider tires, whereas convertibles were built without flares. Two red Sebring-style hash marks were painted on the driver-side front fender. The Grand Sport option was inspired by the five Grand Sport models built in 1963 that last saw racing competition in 1966.

Yet another small-block 350-ci V-8, the LT4, was developed exclusively for the 1996 Corvette. Rated at 330 horsepower, it featured a higher compression ratio, a new aluminum head design, a new camshaft profile, and roller rocker arms. The LT4 was standard on the Grand Sport and optional on other models but only with six-speed manual transmissions. LT1s were used exclusively with automatic transmissions, which offered better shift quality and improved torque converters. Both the LT4 and LT1 sported a new throttle body.

Special embroidery on the seats and special badges signified Collector Edition models.

Price: $36,785 coupe, $43,665 convertible

Engines: 350-ci 300-/330-horsepower V-8

Transmissions: Four-speed automatic, six-speed manual

Total production: 21,536 (17,167 coupes; 4,369 convertibles)

Fact: Only 1,000 Grand Sports (746 coupes and 254 convertibles) were produced, making them very collectible.

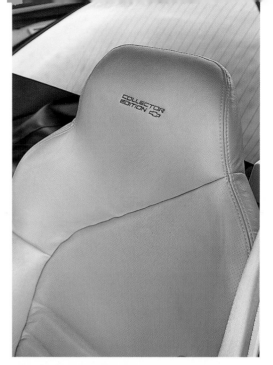

The 350-ci LT4 engine, developed exclusively for the 1996 Corvette, pumped out 330 horses.

1997–2004

Chapter 5

Nineteen ninety-seven was another major milestone in Corvette history; the C5, or fifth-generation, Corvette was released. The sleek new model, available only as a coupe, was equipped with a new small-block V-8 engine. Dubbed the LS1, the new V-8 put out 345 horsepower. Only a little more than 9,000 were produced for the debut year, and it was an unqualified success with demand so strong for the new Corvette that many dealers commanded—and got—several thousand dollars over the sticker price from buyers who just *had* to have one.

In 1998, a convertible was offered along with the coupe, and C5 popularity continued to skyrocket as production jumped to over 31,000 units for the coupe and ragtop combined.

Nineteen ninety-nine saw the debut of a third body style for Corvette—the fixed-roof coupe—and the availability of a head-up display (HUD) option that projected key instrumentation read-outs on the windshield, allowing drivers to view vital information without taking their eyes off the road.

In 2001, base horsepower for the Corvette increased to 350, up 5 horsepower from previous years, and the new super Corvette, the Z06, was introduced with a whopping 385-horsepower LS6 engine. However, this new balls-to-the-wall performance version was only offered in the fixed-roof coupe body style since the tremendous amount of torque it generated was too great for the inherent chassis flex of convertibles.

Body styles remained unchanged through 2004, the last year of the C5s. Minor options and color choices were offered during the last three years of its production.

The 1997 Corvette, available only in coupe body style, was totally new from the ground up.

The C5 was the most thoroughly new Corvette in the model's 40-plus-year history. Rather than fiberglass, the new body was made of a flexible, sheet-molded composite compound (SMC). The trademark fender gills, located behind the front wheelwell to draw off engine heat, were offset by a cove that ran the length of the door—reminiscent of one of the car's earliest styling features.

Under the skin, structural integrity was improved while using one-third fewer components for fewer squeaks and rattles. The 1997 chassis rails were hydroformed, a process that exposes rounded seamless steel to enormous hydraulic pressure to precisely bend and shape the desired form from a single length of tubing. The light yet rigid frame allows better handling and a quieter, smoother ride.

The engine was the third manifestation of Corvette's small-block overhead-valve V-8. Called the LS1, the 350-ci 345-horsepower engine was 44 pounds lighter than the 1996 LT4. Another first for the 1997 Corvette was a rear transaxle with a torque tube connecting the engine to the rear-mounted transmission. Combined with an electronically controlled four-speed automatic transmission or a six-speed manual, front-to-rear weight distribution was nearly equalized.

Everything about the new C5 used cutting-edge technology, from the hydroformed chassis rails to the SMC body. With less than 10,000 produced, demand far surpassed supply, so dealers had a field day charging and getting whatever they wanted for the new Corvettes.

The C5's interior was ergonomically designed and roomier than the C4's.

Price: $37,495

Engines: 350-ci 345-horsepower V-8

Transmissions: Four-speed automatic, six-speed manual

Total production: 9,752 coupes only

Fact: A balsa wood/composite plastic sandwich for the floor of the passenger cockpit served to dampen road noise and vibration.

My wife's C5 screamer is wearing its nose mask and removable aftermarket hardtop that gives it a real Z06 look. *Tom Benford*

In 1998, the Corvette was once again available as both a coupe and a convertible. Standard features included dual air bags, a three-point safety belt system, and daytime running lights.

Price: **$37,995 coupe, $44,425 convertible**

Engines: 350-ci 345-horsepower V-8

Transmissions: Automatic, six-speed manual

Total production: 31,084 (19,235 coupes; 11,849 convertibles)

Fact: This was the first time a Corvette convertible was equipped with a heated, glass rear window.

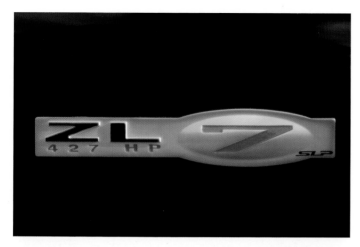

After all the SLP ZL7 modifications were completed, the car was dyno tested before the 427-horsepower fender badges were installed. My wife, Liz, drives the car daily for shopping and other tasks as well as for pleasure driving. It's extremely reliable and very civilized for normal driving, but things get crazy in a hurry when you step on the pedal. *Tom Benford*

Go-fast Corvettes need stop-fast brakes to match, so a set of oversized Baer Eradi-Speed cryogenically treated, drilled-and-slotted rotors with four-piston calipers and aggressive ceramic pads at all four corners were installed, along with a set of chromed Z06 wheels. *Tom Benford*

Other cabin modifications included a billet shifter knob, XM Satellite Radio, a head-up display retrofit (HUD was not available until 1999), logo floor mats, a glare-killing dash mat, and some other goodies for comfortable cruising. *Tom Benford*

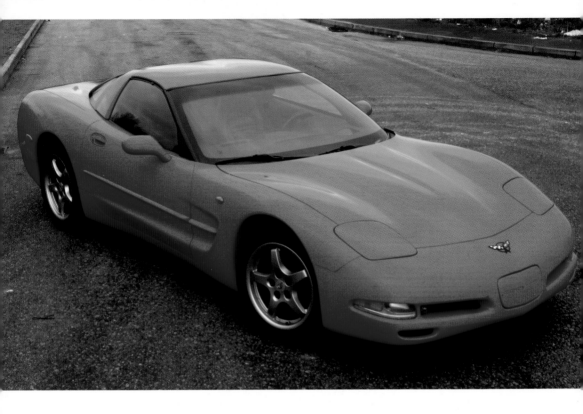

The 1999 Corvette coupe looked identical to the two previous years.

The hardtop model arrived for 1999, the first fixed-roof Corvette offered since the second-generation Sting Rays of 1963–1967. The hardtop joined the coupe (with removable roof panel) and the convertible, and it was aimed at the bargain-conscious potential Corvette buyer.

New options for 1999 included the head-up display (HUD), a twilight sentinel that delayed shutoff of the headlamps allowing exterior illumination after the ignition was turned off, and a power telescoping steering column—but these options were only available on the coupe and convertible, not on the new hardtop.

Price: $38,770 hardtop, $39,171 coupe, $45,579 convertible

Engines: 350-ci 345-horsepower V-8

Transmissions: Four-speed automatic, six-speed manual

Total production: 33,270 (4,031 hardtops; 18,078 coupes; 11,161 convertibles)

Fact: Not feeling that the hardtop was a true Corvette since it was aimed at the budget buyer, its elitist detractors dubbed the hardtop the "Billy Bob."

The 350-ci LS1 engine's output remained at 345 horsepower with no options, unchanged from the debut of the C5 in 1997.

The big new option for 1999 was the head-up display (HUD), which projected vital engine info onto the windshield. *Tom Benford collection*

The selective ride control option permitted the driver to dial up the desired degree of softness or firmness of the ride.

New five-spoke forged-aluminum wheels, available with an optional high-polish finish, were the only new standard equipment added to the 2000 models, and all three—coupe, convertible, and hardtop—looked identical to the 1999 editions. Additional standard performance features included heavy-duty vented four-wheel disc brakes with ABS, electronic throttle control, traction control, Goodyear Eagle extended-mobility performance tires, and a tire pressure monitor system.

The active handling system was available as an option on all three models. This system worked in conjunction with the ABS and traction control systems to selectively apply any of the four brakes in an effort to help the driver counteract potentially dangerous handling characteristics, such as severe oversteer or understeer.

Five-spoke forged-aluminum wheels, available with the optional high-polish finish shown here, were standard equipment for all 2000 Corvettes.

Price: $38,900 hardtop, $39,475 coupe, $45,900 convertible

Engines: 350-ci 345-horsepower V-8

Transmissions: Four-speed automatic, six-speed manual

Total production: 33,682 (2,090 hardtops; 18,113 coupes; 13,479 convertibles)

Fact: Lagging sales and bad press made this the last year of the Billy Bob hardtop, but that body style wasn't quite dead yet.

The interior of the car, as well as what was under the hood, remained the same for 2000 as in previous years.

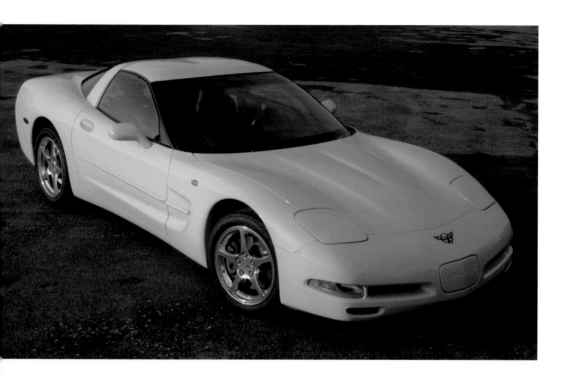

Aside from additional exterior color choices, the 2000 Corvettes were carbon copies of the 1999 models in all three body styles.

The coupe remained the favorite of the three body styles, with 18,113 of them made and sold in 2000.

Chevrolet scored a real winner with the C5, so it saw no good reason to deviate from a winning formula; hence, the 2001 Corvette bore no discernable exterior changes from its predecessors.

For the 2001 model year, the Billy Bob hardtop model was dead, but the new, high-performance Z06 hardtop was now the baddest kid on the block—and it used the same body! The standard LS1 Corvette engine was coaxed to output 5 additional horses, raising the output to 350 horsepower thanks to a new camshaft profile.

The new Z06 was specifically designed for high performance, with its LS6 engine putting out 385 horsepower. The hardtop body was sufficiently rigid to handle the torque and power of the more powerful motor, hence it was adopted for the Z06 model.

Price: $47,500 Z06 hardtop, $40,475 coupe, $47,000 convertible

Engines: 350-ci 350-horsepower V-8; 350-ci 385-horsepower (Z06)

Transmissions: Automatic, six-speed manual

Total production: 35,627 (5,773 Z06 hardtops; 15,681 coupes; 14,173 convertibles)

Fact: Both the LS1 and LS6 engines were equipped with new intake manifolds made of a nylon composite material that provided better breathing.

The lower vents and grille openings endow the nose of the car with a sharklike appearance in keeping with the Corvette heritage and legacy started with the Mid-Year Sting Rays.

Aimed at buyers looking for an unbridled, truly aggressive Corvette that rekindled the visceral adrenaline rush last felt with the big-block Sting Rays of yesteryear, the 2001 Z06 put 385 horses at the driver's disposal, but this was only the beginning of the new super Corvette era. *Tom Benford collection*

The Z06 really became the super Corvette with a power boost that brought it up to 405 horsepower in 2002.

The really big news for 2002 was the 20-horsepower boost on the Z06, bringing it up to a whopping 405 horsepower right off the showroom floor, and the head-up display (HUD) was now standard equipment on the super Corvette as well.

Other new items included a standard AM/FM stereo with in-dash CD player on the coupe and convertible, and the navy blue metallic and dark Bowling Green metallic exterior colors were canceled.

Price: $50,150 Z06 hardtop, $41,450 coupe, $47,975 convertible

Engines: 350-ci 350-horsepower V-8; 350-ci 405-horsepower V-8 (Z06)

Transmissions: Automatic, six-speed manual

Total production: 35,767 (8,297 Z06 hardtops; 14,760 coupes; 12,710 convertibles)

Fact: For 2002, the automatic transmission cooler case was constructed of lightweight cast aluminum that replaced the previous stainless-steel design.

The black-trimmed brake vents ahead of the rear wheels on the Z06 are actually functional rather than just decorative touches.

The Z06 wheels were cast aluminum, rather than forged aluminum, for 2002.

The LS1 350-ci engine remained at 350 horsepower for 2003.

Indeed, 2003 was a milestone year for the Corvette. And to celebrate its 50th anniversary, a special 50th Anniversary Edition was available in both coupe and convertible configurations, designated by Anniversary Red paint and special badges both inside and out.

Other news for the Corvette's golden anniversary included standard foglamps, sport seats, a power passenger seat, dual-zone auto HVAC (coupe and convertible), a parcel net, and a luggage shade (coupe).

Price: $51,155 Z06 hardtop, $43,895 coupe, $50,370 convertible

Engines: 350-ci 350-horsepower V-8; 350-ci 405-horsepower V-8 (Z06)

Transmissions: Automatic, six-speed manual

Total production: 35,469 (8,635 Z06 hardtops; 12,812 coupes; 14,022 convertibles)

Fact: During 2003 only, all Corvettes featured a special 50th Anniversary emblem on the front and rear. The emblem was silver and had the number "50" with the signature cross-flag design.

All 2003 Corvettes, regardless of model, received the 50th Anniversary commemorative front and rear emblems.

The foglamps inside the front grille vents were a new piece of standard equipment for the 2003 edition.

The basic body styles for all models—coupe, hardtop, Z06, and convertible—didn't undergo any changes for 2003.

The Corvette C5-R victories at Le Mans and other tracks made the world sit up and take notice. The commemorative edition of the Z06 had the same effect on the street.

Owing to the Corvette C5-R's remarkable racing success at Le Mans and other tracks, the 2004 Corvettes, which were the last of the C5s, were available in special Le Mans commemorative editions with distinctive red-white-and-blue color schemes.

Price: $52,385 Z06 hardtop, $44,535 coupe, $51,535 convertible

Engines: 350-ci 350-horsepower V-8; 350-ci 405-horsepower V-8 (Z06)

Transmissions: Automatic, six-speed manual

Total production: 34,064 (5,683 Z06 hardtops; 16,165 coupes; 12,216 convertibles)

Fact: The Z06 commemorative edition was equipped with a new lightweight carbon-fiber hood.

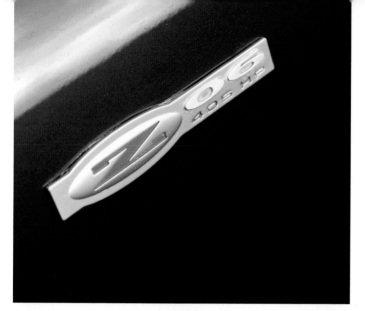

Lest there be any mistake, the Z06 fender badges tell it like it is. When you've got it, flaunt it.

Commemorative badges adorned all of these special editions, and the Z06 had a new lightweight carbon-fiber hood to celebrate the occasion.

With 405-horsepower output, the Z06 LS6 engine was a force to be reckoned with.

2005 and Beyond

Chapter 6

The C6—the current generation of Corvette—was released for the 2005 model year in both coupe and convertible formats. The new generation debuted with an LS2 6-liter V-8 that delivered 400 horsepower and 400 lb-ft of torque right off the showroom floor, thus making it the most powerful Corvette ever offered in standard, pure-stock trim. The new C6 also had exposed headlights for the first time in 42 years, and, with a 0.28 drag coefficient, the C6 was the most aerodynamically efficient Corvette ever.

For the 2006 model year, the awesome 505-horsepower Z06 was unleashed on the sports car world, making it the fastest and most technologically advanced production model up to that point in the Corvette's 54-year history. Other changes for 2006 Corvettes across the board included a smaller-diameter steering wheel, a six-speed automatic trans for both the coupe and convertible (the Z06 was available only with six-speed manual trans), and the inclusion of XM satellite radio in concert with the up-level Bose audio system for all Corvettes sold in the 48 contiguous states. Assorted new exterior colors and a new Titanium Grey interior color were also hallmarks of the 2006 Corvette.

For 2007, the convertible received a power top as standard equipment rather than optional as it had been formerly, and across the board the new Corvette models received larger glove boxes. With a top speed of 186 miles per hour and other performance enhancements, the 2007 Corvette could rightly be called a supercar without any exaggeration. And the end is not in sight as the engineers who work on the Corvette continually improve America's sports car.

The sixth generation of Corvettes, the C6s, achieved a great blend of technical sophistication with expressive style. Five inches shorter than the C5, the 2005 Corvette cuts a tighter, tauter profile with virtually no loss of usable space. And with a 0.28 drag coefficient, the new Corvette was the most aerodynamically efficient Corvette ever.

The new LS2 6.0-liter small-block V-8 was the standard engine in the 2005 Corvette, delivering 400 horsepower and 400 lb-ft. of torque. It was the largest, most powerful standard small-block engine ever offered in Corvette.

Five inches shorter overall, the C6 maintained the bobbed tail section that started with the Sharks back in 1968.

Price: $44,245 coupe, $52,245 convertible

Engines: 364-ci 400-horsepower V-8

Transmissions: Automatic, six-speed manual

Total production: 37,372 (26,728 coupes; 10,644 convertibles)

Fact: The removable roof panel of the C6 was 15 percent larger yet offered the same structural stiffness as that of the C5, while weighing just one pound more.

The new Corvette got a new engine, too, with the LS2. At 364-ci displacement, it was the largest production small-block ever to go in a Corvette. And at 400 horsepower, it was the most powerful standard Corvette engine ever.

The C6 interior is a bit roomier and definitely more luxurious than the C5's, and GPS/DVD players are among the many available goodies.

Even the disc brake calipers are unmistakably identified as uniquely Corvette.

The functional rear brake vents took on a scoop-type shape for the 2006 Z06, while the trademark Corvette coves were retained on all C6 models.

Two thousand six was like old-home week for the Corvette: the Z06 returned to the Corvette lineup, and what a return it made, equipped with the new LS7 427-ci V-8 that outputs an incredible 505 horsepower. So it was also a return of the fabled 427-ci Corvette engine as well.

Other noteworthy news for the 2006 coupe and convertible models included the availability of a new electronically controlled six-speed paddle-shift transmission with automatic modes and a new three-spoke, 9.4-inch-diameter steering wheel that allows the driver to maintain a tighter feel on the wheel and help improve turn-in response.

Price: $65,000 Z06 hardtop, $43,500 coupe, $51,535 convertible

Engines: 364-ci 400-horsepower V-8; 427-ci 505-horsepower V-8 (Z06)

Transmissions: Six-speed paddle-shift automatic, six-speed manual

Total production: 34,021 (16,598 coupes; 11,151 convertibles; 6,272 Z06 hardtops)

Fact: The 2006 Corvettes were equipped with an automatic passenger-sensing system that turned off the passenger air bag if there was no passenger in the car, thereby preventing passenger air bag deployment in the event of a collision.

The 427-ci LS7 engine brings back fond memories of Sting Rays of the same displacement when cubic inches and horsepower reigned supreme.

The almost-vertical rear fascia has become a modern trademark of the C6 and the view most other cars get of a new Corvette on the road.

For those who are doubters, the Z06 fender badges tell it like it is—505 ponies under the hood.

Massive drilled rotors and humongous calipers ensure the Z06's stopping power is equal to its acceleration and speed.

The C6 door handles were changed to an edge-mounted arrangement for a sleeker appearance.

The functional small scoop on the nose of the Z06 is reminiscent of the stinger hood of the 1967 big-block Sting Rays. Since the cars had 427-ci engines in common, the tribute is quite fitting.

Special Cars

Chapter 7

For more than a half century, the Corvette has quickened pulses, created excitement, sparked imaginations, and frequently given physical form to the possibilities of what could be. It is both the destiny and legacy of the Corvette to always be something more than just a car; indeed, as America's Sports Car it is symbolic of freedom—freedom to be different, unique, individual. Along the way, there were several truly special Corvettes that dared to go forth on uncharted ground. This section is devoted to these special cars and to the memory of the individuals responsible for creating them.

The EX 122, sporting red paint, a 265-ci V-8, and the full-length spear/hash visited the National Corvette Museum in Bowling Green, Kentucky, when then owner Jack Ingle loaned it to the institution. *Tom Benford*

EX 122—the Corvette dream car that took the spotlight on the turntable at the Waldorf-Astoria Hotel in New York City at GM's January 1953 Motorama show—is the prototype Corvette and the progenitor of all Corvettes that followed.

The production 1953 Corvettes were copies of the EX 122 Motorama car with very few changes. After Corvette production started in late June 1953 in the Flint, Michigan, plant, EX 122 was sent back to Detroit, where it sat in the lobby of GM's design center for several months. Engineering took custody of the car and used it as a test mule for the new 265-ci V-8 engine. EX 122 was then used as a Chevrolet courtesy car for about 5,000 miles before being put up for sale. Russell Sanders, who was in charge of GM's experimental division at the time, purchased it on April 11, 1956, for an unknown price (some speculate it may have been $1).

The car was used extensively by Sanders' family for several years, until he sold it to Jack

EX 122 had hinged headlight grilles, whereas the production cars did not. As with numerous other one-off parts, George Kerbeck had these hand-fabricated from the original blueprints for the restoration. *Tom Benford*

The original Blue Flame Special six-cylinder engine that was in EX 122 for the 1953 Motorama was replaced with a 265-ci V-8 while the car was being used as a test mule. The V-8 became standard equipment for the Corvette beginning with the 1955 model year. *Tom Benford*

The restored EX 122 on display at Corvettes at Carlisle in 2004. Compare this with photos of production 1953 Corvettes, and you'll see the subtle differences. *Tom Benford*

Ingle for $1,000 on October 10, 1959. The car stayed in Ingle's possession for many years, and it was shown at Bloomington, Meadow Brook Hall, and other high-profile automobile shows until Jack Ingle passed away in 2001. George Kerbeck acquired EX 122 in July 2002 from the Ingle estate and restored it to the way it was on the stage of the Waldorf more than a half century ago.

To Corvette aficionados, EX 122 is like the Holy Grail—it's the one that started it all, and because of that fact, it holds a very important place in automotive history in general and Corvette history in particular.

There are some who doubt the authenticity of EX 122, citing the original Motorama car had a Blue Flame Special six-cylinder engine, whereas Kerbeck's car has a 265-ci V-8

The red interior was standard along with the Polo White exterior color scheme for all 1953 Corvettes, just as it was for the Motorama show car. *Tom Benford*

under its hood, as purchased. Also, prior to the restoration, it had the long production spear hash facing upward, no outside door buttons, nonhinged headlight guards, and it was red—all different from what was shown at the 1953 Motorama. Kerbeck thought about putting the six-banger back in the car and displaying the V-8 on a stand with appropriate signage. Keeping the V-8 in it and displaying a Blue Flame Special on a stand was also considered, but Kerbeck's final decision was that it left GM with the V-8 in it, so that's how it should stay.

EX 122 is on display in the showroom of Kerbeck Chevrolet in Atlantic City for all to see and to pay homage to the little car that started it all.

Legend has it that Jerry Earl, son of GM styling chief Harley Earl, yearned to race a Ferrari—something that wouldn't sit too well with the GM powers-that-be from a PR standpoint. Although Chevrolet already had the 1956 Sebring racers in their stable, to keep Jerry from jumping on the Ferrari bandwagon, Harley Earl had his designers come up with a hotter-looking Corvette for his son to race; the SR-2 was the result.

Resembling the original SR-2 racer in many respects, upon closer inspection one can tell this is, in reality, a modified 1958 (C1) Corvette. The washboard hood was only used on the 1958 Corvette, and the original SR-2 was built in 1956.

Here's the rear view of the SR-2 copy. The original is on permanent display in the National Corvette Museum in Bowling Green, Kentucky.

This racer is a converted production 1963 split-window coupe with its bumpers removed, additional vent holes cut into the lower rear fascia, and other modifications for track use.

A policy memo issued on January 21, 1963, reiterated the company's compliance with the 1957 AMA company-sponsored racing ban issued by then GM chairman Frederic Donner. The memo officially canceled production plans for the Corvette Grand Sport, with only 5 of the intended 125 cars built. But, there was no shortage of independent racers who chose the Corvette as their vehicle of choice in their quests to capture the checkered flags.

Although the original factory-built Grand Sports looked similar to production Corvette coupes, in reality they had nothing in common, since their fiberglass bodies were only about half as thick as production bodies and they had handmade tubular-steel chassis to save weight. Their aggressive styling and impressive performance characteristics, however, inspired many independent racers to adopt the Grand Sport look, and the 1963 split-window coupe often received full-blown track modifications.

If you're going to emulate a true legend of the racetrack, then one of the original Grand Sports is certainly a great model, right down to the No. 65 and the red/white/blue color scheme. Note the passenger-side mirror added to overcome the blind spot caused by the split of the rear window—a solution that nobody thought of at GM back in 1963 when the split rear window caused such turmoil and controversy.

The five-spoke mag wheels and side exhausts are all functional modifications for the track, as is the vent hole cut into the fender behind the wheelwell. While the Sting Ray design was beautiful to look at, it had very bad aerodynamics, which causes the front end to lift at speed; this vent hole was undoubtedly cut to alleviate such problems.

The CERV I as it looks today, fully restored. *Tom Benford collection*

CERV I stands for "Chevrolet Engineering Research Vehicle" number one. CERV I was the darling of the first Corvette chief engineer, Zora Arkus-Duntov. It was used as a test bed for the independent suspension geometry that was introduced in production 1963 Corvettes. It was also an engineering test bed for powertrains, receiving seven engines for testing over its lifetime. The seventh (which is still installed) is a 377-ci all-aluminum Grand Sport Corvette engine of which only six were ever made. The fuel injection is a one-of-a-kind-design Hilborn-type unit.

The seven 377 blocks were specially cast by Alcoa for Chevrolet in 1963 at a staggering cost of $284,000 for all seven. With this special engine, toward the end of the car's test life at Chevrolet, CERV I rounded the oval test track at Milford, Michigan, at over 204 miles per hour. It would be 10 years before any vehicle achieved that speed at Indianapolis.

CERV I was designed in 1960 by Larry Shinoda, who was also the accredited designer of the 1963 Corvette split-window coupe. The CERV I's dry weight is 1,650 pounds, its bare chrome-moly frame weight is 125 pounds, and its bare fiberglass body weighs a mere 80 pounds. It was the first vehicle to have rubber safety foam-filled fuel bladders (two 10-gallon tanks mounted on its sides); it was also a test bed for the Firestone tire company. The vehicle is currently owned by Mike Yager, chief cheerleader of Mid America Motorworks, a major supplier of Corvette parts and accessories based in Effingham, Illinois.

The CERV I prior to its restoration. Note the heat discoloration on the headers. *Tom Benford collection*

Zora Arkus-Duntov behind the wheel of the CERV I at Daytona Beach International Speedway, taken on Sunday, February 26, 1961. *Tom Benford collection*

The CERV I on display as part of owner Mike Yager's My Garage Collection at Mid America Motorworks. *Tom Benford collection*

It started out as a standard L84 fuel-injected coupe when it was taken off the assembly line and customized to Bill Mitchell's personal tastes. *Tom Benford collection*

Known for its radical dream cars, Chevrolet decided to build a more mainstream creation for the auto shows and the World's Fair of New York in 1964. This red L84 fuel-injected coupe was transferred from the assembly line in St. Louis and modified by the GM Tech Center as Shop Order 10361.

Its numerous special features include an enlarged grille opening, special large side exhausts and mirrors, a cut-out hood, and 16 coats of gold-base candy apple red lacquer paint with matching interior. The seat backs were extended to incorporate headrests; the console is in matching iridescent red leather, as are the door panels, which have brushed stainless-steel panels. The side pipes are one of a kind and are machined from a solid stainless-steel casting.

Larry Shinoda lent his talents to the effort by adding rear brake vents (purely cosmetic) and special side-inset fiberglass treatments. The car also has polished stainless toe board grilles, handmade emblems, and a cast egg-crate grille. The special cast, ribbed fuel-injection unit's cover extends through the hood, which was filled and modified for a cleaner look in 1965. The engine compartment was custom finished and heavily chromed. The car is now part of the My Garage Collection of Mike Yager of Mid America Motorworks in Effingham, Illinois.

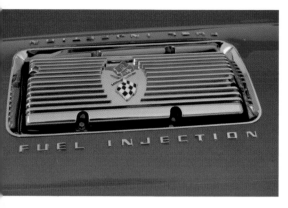

The chromed, ribbed, specially cast cover of the fuel-injection unit pokes through the hood. *Tom Benford collection*

The purely cosmetic rear brake vents were one of Shinoda's ideas, as was the one-off gas filler door design. Neither idea ever made it into production. *Tom Benford collection*

Matching red iridescent leather upholstery complements the candy apple red paint, accented by lots of chrome and stainless brightwork. *Tom Benford collection*

The gauge cluster has been stripped of paint and polished, along with chrome-plated rims on the gauges. The odometer shows 28,690 miles. Wonder who could have racked up all those miles—GM head of styling Bill Mitchell or Mike Yager, its current owner? *Tom Benford collection*

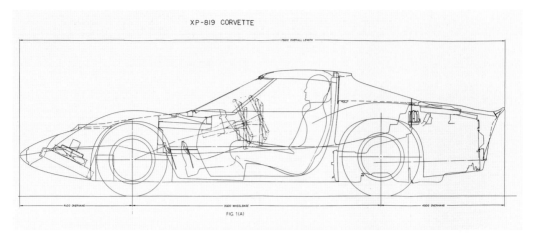

XP-819 CORVETTE

FIG 1(A)

This is one of the original engineering drawings of the XP-819, showing relative component/driver positioning. *Tom Benford collection*

An early side view of the XP-819; compare this to the engineering drawing. *Tom Benford collection*

XP-819 was the responsibility of Frank Winchell, the chief of Chevrolet R&D from 1960. Winchell moved up the ranks from the Power Train Transmission division, and he was noted for his experimental work in transaxle assemblies and front-wheel-drive units. Winchell's craftsmen and engineers were working very closely with Jim Hall and the behind-the-scenes Chaparral program. Larry Shinoda designed the body of XP-819 as well as the take-apart aluminum wheels—the same wheels found on Hall's Chaparrals. XP-819 development was introduced to Chevrolet management in April 1966 under the auspices of safety, but it was really a means for Winchell to pursue his dream of a rear-engine production sports car—ostensibly, the future Corvette.

XP-819 was the first car to utilize electrically powered control pedals, found today on Cadillacs and the Ford Taurus. The XP-819 has special

The rear-mounted engine was Winchell's vision for the future of the Corvette and vehemently opposed by Arkus-Duntov. *Tom Benford collection*

crash barriers molded into the doors, and it was the first use of urethane in molded bumper construction. The specially designed steering column telescopes and would collapse in case of a collision. It is connected to the first use of rack-and-pinion steering in a Chevrolet, the same design used in Hall's Chaparrals (rack-and-pinion was not seen in production until 1984). The engine is a reverse-rotation 327-ci 350-horsepower small-block with large valve heads and a special gear-drive timing system. The transaxle is one-of-a-kind 1963 Pontiac Tempest valve body combined with a unique housing utilizing Oldsmobile special-design half shafts. The front and rear suspension are prototypes and unique to the car.

XP-819 was the Corvette that would never be; erratic handling at high speeds and other dynamic characteristics put it out of the running. After GM disposed of XP-819 in 1969, it was stored in Smokey Yunick's paint booth for over 20 years until a Chevrolet dealer from Missouri discovered the car, which was subsequently acquired by Mike Yager for his My Garage Collection at Mid America Motorworks. It is currently undergoing restoration.

The interior of XP-819 was a study in driver and passenger safety engineering with form-fitting seats, an energy-absorbing steering column, and other innovations. *Tom Benford collection*

The XP-897 GT was thought to be the shape of things to come for the Corvette, but this was a widely held misconception.

Built on an early Porsche 914 platform by Pininfarina in Italy to GM's design, the XP-897 GT Two-Rotor car was built to prove (or disprove) the viability of a Corvette powered by a two-rotor engine. Ultimately, it proved to be underpowered and convinced GM management that a Wankel-powered Corvette would have to use a four-rotor engine. Still, XP-897 was shown in 1973 as a showcase for GM's then imminent Wankel-type rotary engine. It was widely believed, though mistakenly so, to be the precursor to the next-generation Corvette. For a number of reasons, the Wankel rotary engine would never power a Corvette, or any GM production car, for that matter.

Styled by Pininfarina for GM, the XP-897 was quite a good-looking car that, unfortunately, never saw the light of day.

The XP-897 was built on a Porsche 914 platform, with the two-rotor Wankel engine mounted amidships (hidden by a hinged cover behind the front seats) and utilizing a transaxle powertrain.

"Garish" is a word that comes to mind and fits the look of the *Corvette Summer* Stingray quite well. Intended to look outrageous, it certainly hits its mark. *Tom Benford collection*

This is the original customized Stingray from the MGM/United Artists movie *Corvette Summer*, starring Mark Hamill and Annie Potts. The car was built by Dick Korkes of Korky's Kustom Studios for MGM. The Corvette was a 1973 Stingray converted to right-hand drive so that Hamill could hang out of the curbside window and chat up the ladies while cruising.

The car is now owned by Mike Yager of Mid America Motorworks and is part of his My Garage Collection.

The sparkle effect behind the red Plexiglas was achieved by crinkling up aluminum foil. *Tom Benford collection*

The Stingray script nestles within the bowtie logo and is set off by the wild metal-flake paint job.
Tom Benford collection

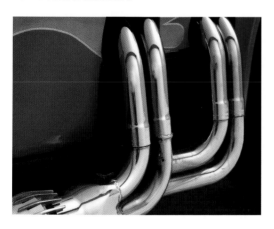

The chrome exhaust headers exit through the fender of the car and contribute to the outrageous look. *Tom Benford collection*

Aside from the right-hand drive, a custom steering wheel, and the relocation of the ignition switch to the center console, the interior is basically stock. To*m Benford collection*

Take a good look: this is the only 1983 Corvette still in existence! *Tom Benford collection*

Due to major production and quality-control problems, no 1983 Corvette was ever released to the public, but that's not to say that none were ever built. In actuality, 44 cars were assembled; these were all pilot cars, and it's estimated that they cost about $500,000 each to fabricate. Pilot cars were used to work out manufacturing bugs and assembly line production problems, assess engineering, and for other such purposes, not the least of which was prerelease publicity.

These pilot cars contained leading-edge technology that promised to make the totally new Corvette a world-class sports car that was head and shoulders above all others. Aside from the Cross-Fire Injection L83 engine and the 700R4 automatic transmission used on the 1982 Corvettes, these 1983 pilot cars were to usher in a totally new Corvette. Of the 44 pilot cars built, 33 were used for crash testing and other purposes by the engineering department, while the remaining 11 cars were used at the Bowling Green plant to evaluate assembly processes.

Originally slated to be released in fall 1982, assembly line problems at Bowling Green coupled with brisk sales of the 1982 Corvette delayed introduction of the new model until March 1983. There were so many quality problems with the prototype 1983 Corvettes, in fact, that by the time the problems were finally corrected to the satisfaction of management, it was too late into the model year and the car was introduced as a 1984 model and was run for a year and a half. These quality-control problems proved to be a real wake-up call, not only to GM, but to virtually every American automobile manufacturer, as foreign imports were winning a constantly expanding share of the U.S. car-buying market due to the better quality and value they delivered.

The 44 1983 Corvettes that were built were virtually identical to the 1984 model that was released. Because of this, all of the pilot cars, except for a single sole survivor, were destroyed. Only serial number 23 was left unscathed, and it was moved to the National Corvette Museum, where it is still on permanent display with slightly less than 10,000 miles on its odometer.

The Corvette Challenge series cars were identical showroom stock Corvettes, with the exception of mandatory optional equipment required by the SCCA for competition. *Tom Benford collection*

Corvettes were expelled from SCCA Showroom Stock competition in the 1980s because they outclassed other cars in performance and technology by such a degree that they were considered to be unfair competition. John Powell of Corvette marketing, however, convinced the SCCA to run a Corvette-only series that limited competition to identical showroom-stock Corvettes. This series was called the Corvette Challenge.

From 1987, the Corvette Challenge cars were available only by special order, and an SCCA license was required to purchase them. These cars included special options for this series

that included a fire-suppression system, an exhaust system without catalytic converters, and a full roll cage.

The Corvette Challenge ran for two years as a series of sprint races in conjunction with other main events. After two seasons, the series was shut down when Powell couldn't come up with sufficient sponsorship money.

The 1988 Corvette Challenge car featured here is currently owned by Mike Yager of Mid America Motorworks in his My Garage Collection. Mid America Motorworks, known in those days as Mid America Designs, was a major sponsor of the Corvette Challenge series.

Aside from the fire-suppression system equipment, the Corvette Challenge cars' interiors were identical to standard production Corvettes, including the stereo systems. *Tom Benford collection*

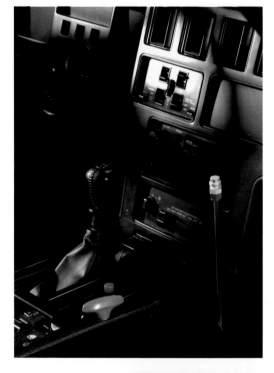

Mid America Motorworks, known as Mid America Designs in the days of the Corvette Challenge, was a sponsor right from the start of the series. *Tom Benford collection*

These special cars had emblems to set them apart from standard production Corvettes. An SCCA license was required to order a Corvette Challenge car. *Tom Benford collection*

The 350-ci engines of the Corvette Challenge cars were equipped with tuned-port fuel injection, just like the other production Corvettes of the day. *Tom Benford collection*

Ever since the first Corvette rolled off the assembly line in 1953, the marque has been favorite fodder for customizers, the author included. It seems that for every Corvette, there's someone with their own particular vision of how to make it better, prettier, faster, or just plain different. Here are some of those ideas, as well as some Corvette things you're not likely to see elsewhere!

The classic stinger hood design of the big-block 1967 Mid-Year Corvette has been adapted by aftermarket accessory manufacturers, and here one perches on a customized Shark. *Tom Benford*

This customized Mid-Year coupe got several coats of C6 Daytona Sunset Orange paint, flush door handles, a full roll cage, lots of performance upgrades, and DUB wheels and tires. *Tom Benford*

Carbon-fiber covers and lots of other eye-candy trick out the engine compartment of this C5. *Tom Benford*

American icons salute each other. Gibson has issued three limited-edition guitars commemorating the Corvette over the years: a Cove Side edition, the Mid-Year edition, and the 50th Anniversary C5 edition. ZZ Top's Billy Gibbons played a 50th Anniversary edition on stage at the Corvette 50th anniversary celebration in Nashville in June 2003. *Tom Benford*

This is not factory stock shifting gear, to be sure.
Tom Benford

In case you were wondering what lurks beneath the hood of this drag-strip Mid-Year.
Tom Benford

Then there are those who really want to take things to the extreme, as in the case of this '65 Mid-Year coupe set up for the drag strip. *Tom Benford*

The museum has dozens of historic Corvettes on display at all times, including the one-millionth Corvette to come off the assembly line. *Tom Benford*

If you were the head of styling for the Corvette as Bill Mitchell was, then you could have a factory-customized Corvette made for your wife, which Mitchell did with this 1976 Shark for Mrs. Mitchell. The body was resculptured by GM design staff under Mitchell's direction and refinished in pearl white, with extensive use of striping and chrome trim. The custom saddle leather interior was later replaced with red factory trim by Mrs. Mitchell after Bill's passing. The drivetrain—composed of an all-aluminum 454-ci Can-Am engine, L88 automatic, and heavy-duty rear axle—was installed by Smokey Yunick. *Tom Benford*

INDEX